DATE DUE

The Simple Guide to
SNORKELING
FUN

T.F.H.

The Simple Guide to

SNORKELING

FUN

Steven M. Barsky

BEST PUBLISHING COMPANY

Photography by Steven M. Barsky unless otherwise indicated.

ISBN: 0-941332-71-3
Library of Congress catalog card number: 98-89448

Composed, printed and bound in the United States of America.

Best Publishing Company
2355 North Steves Boulevard
P.O. Box 30100
Flagstaff, Arizona 86003-0100 USA

Acknowledgments

Most of the books I have written have been suggested to me by friends in the diving business. Even though my name is the one on the cover of this book, everyone that you see mentioned here was part of making this project happen.

This book was the idea of Steve Holmgren of Best Publishing who saw a need for a text like this. Jim Joiner, my publisher, saw the merit of this work as well and gave this project the green light. Linda Longnaker at Best did the layout for the book and always maintains a great sense of humor, even under tight deadlines and with numerous edits.

Snorkeling is an equipment-dependent sport and many companies assisted us by supplying gear for us to use. Both Dave Stancil and Tom Phillipp at Aqua Lung (formerly U.S. Divers Co., Inc.) have always made available whatever gear we needed for a particular photo session. We also received tremendous assistance from Larry Hagebusch and Richard Skelly at Tabata (TUSA) and from Milka Pejovic-Roller at Scubapro. Allan Edmund at Henderson Aquatics helped us secure their sharp looking dive skins for both children and adults.

Special thanks goes to my friends Bob and Suzanne Evans at Force Fins. Not only did they provide the kid's fins for the family photo session, but Bob also provided numerous photos for this book. There are few people in the diving industry who are as creative as Bob, with his hands, his mind, and his photographic eye.

Photographic equipment was provided by Jeff Mondle at Sea and Sea Photographic and Jens Rubschlager of Sea

Life Cameras. Both these companies make great camera systems for snorkelers. James Forté, U.S. manager for Subal camera housings and Sea Optics, also helped us with gear and is always an excellent source of photographic systems information. Eric Squires at Light and Motion Video Systems furnished a photo of their hot new Mako video housing.

The tropical photos in this book were all shot at Grand Cayman Island, one of the finest snorkeling spots in the world. I have been to very few dive spots where I would want to return, but Grand Cayman is right up there at the top of my list. It can't be beat for great snorkeling, diving, accommodations, friendliness, and convenience.

Our diving on Grand Cayman was with Ron Kipp's Bob Soto's Diving Ltd. Ron is one of the most enthusiastic people in the diving business and always has a positive "can-do" attitude. His operation is one of the most professional I have seen and his dive guides are all superb.

Ron Kipp's crew included managers Barrie Day and Leslie McLain who helped us with our daily logistics, making sure we were always on the right boat and coordinating the technical side of our shoot. Aboard the boats, dive guides Robin Johnsen, Brad Kipp, Andy Kronick, Brad Nelson, Albert Rosendahl, Sandy Sondrol, and Paul Stanton took the time to look after our special needs. There is no better group of dive guides and wonderful, friendly people.

Randy Pringle of Treasure Island Resort assisted us with accommodations and logistics. Treasure Island is a "diver friendly" resort, well located, clean, and comfortable. It's an ideal place for divers and snorkelers.

Many divers, friends, and family took the time to help us with photographs including Kristine Barsky, John

Coudray, the Minderhouts (Aaron, Cory, Dirk, and Karen), Morgan and Walter Wehtje, Lily Lethbridge, Blair Mott, Matt Newnham, and Ed Stetson. Without this group this book could not have been completed.

Additional photos in this book have been provided by some great underwater photographers. On the pages here you'll see the work of Jesse Cancelmo, Ben Cropp, Brad Doane, Bob Evans, Pete Haaker, and Doug Perrine. These are all people who spend hundreds of hours in the water each year to capture the best in underwater photography.

Two of my friends who reviewed the manuscript and provided critical comments were Bob Christensen and Dr. Hugh Greer, M.D. A former commercial diver and avid sport diver, Bob's gentle wisdom and sense of humor has always been an inspiration to me. Dr. Greer, who is considered one of the top diving medical authorities in the country, as well as an accomplished diver and author in his own right, can always be counted on for his insights into diving.

Finally, nothing that I do could be accomplished without the love, support, and participation of my wife, Kristine, who is always at my side. Kristine is one of the most competent divers I know and her mark is on every page of this book. As we dive the seas of the world together, she provides the energy that lets me succeed.

Steve Barsky
Santa Barbara, California
January 1999

WARNING

Any time you enter water deeper than you can stand, you expose yourself to certain risks, the most common of which is drowning. To participate in snorkeling and skin diving (diving without air tanks) you must be a competent swimmer with a reasonable level of physical fitness. Swimming in the ocean, rivers, or lakes presents additional risks due to the effects of boating traffic, marine life, wind, waves, water temperatures, currents, and surf. As a snorkeler or skin diver you must observe and obey directions from any local lifeguards or authorities whenever you enter the water. If you feel tired, cold, or stressed in any way, it is essential to exit the water as soon as possible.

This book is not a substitute for qualified instruction in snorkeling or skin diving. For practical instruction in snorkeling or skin diving, contact a certified diving instructor.

Other Books By Steve Barsky

Careers in Diving
 - with Kristine Barsky and Ronnie Damico

Small Boat Diving

Spearfishing for Skin and Scuba Divers

The Simple Guide to Rebreather Diving
 - with Mark Thurlow and Mike Ward

The Dry Suit Diving Manual

Diving in High-Risk Environments

Dry Suit Diving
 - with Dick Long and Bob Stinton

Diving with the EXO-26® Full Face Mask

Diving with Divator MKII Full Face Mask

Adventures in Scuba Diving

Table of Contents

CHAPTER 1

SNORKELING AND SKIN DIVING

Snorkeling, or swimming on the surface with mask, fins, and snorkel, is one of the most relaxing and interesting activities that you can enjoy. With a mask on your face, you can see down into the depths, and watch dolphins and fish swimming, sea fans waving, and lobsters and crabs crawling along the ocean floor. With a snorkel (breathing tube), you can breathe without lifting your head out of the water, allowing you to float effortlessly on the surface. With fins, you can swim quickly and efficiently, covering a large area with a minimum of effort.

One of the big advantages to snorkeling and skin diving is that without scuba gear, you don't produce noisy bubbles which can frighten many types of marine life. In many cases, a quiet snorkeler or skin diver can get much closer to certain types of marine life than a scuba diver is capable of doing. It's also easier to cover long distances in the water when you're not wearing scuba gear.

Mask, fins, and snorkel are the three most basic items of diving equipment that can be used whether you choose to remain on the surface to make your underwater discoveries or whether you plan to plunge into the depths. You can use this same gear no matter where your diving adventures take you, from the shallowest seas to the deepest shipwrecks.

What is snorkeling?

Snorkeling is swimming on the surface of the water with mask, fins, and snorkel. Almost anyone can participate in snorkeling, provided that they can swim reasonably well, are comfortable in the water, and have a minimum level of physical fitness. It is not necessary to dive underwater to enjoy snorkeling.

Snorkeling is swimming on the surface with mask, fins, and snorkel. You do not need to go underwater to enjoy snorkeling.

(Photo © Bob Evans. La Mer Bleu Productions.)

Snorkeling is the least expensive way to participate in exploring the underwater world. It can be done with a minimum investment in equipment. You will enjoy snorkeling anywhere the water is clear enough and shallow enough for you to see the features of the site you want to view.

However, this doesn't necessarily mean you must see the bottom to enjoy snorkeling. For example, in some parts of the world, people swim with whales in water that is hundreds of feet deep, where the bottom can't be seen, but the water is clear enough to easily watch the whales.

Participating in snorkeling is a good way to see if you are interested in going further and participating in skin or scuba diving. You may decide that you're only interested in snorkeling, or you may find that snorkeling opens a "deeper" interest in exploring underwater.

Instruction is not required for snorkeling, but it is suggested. A snorkeling instructor can show you how to get the most out of your equipment as well as little tricks and techniques for making your snorkeling more enjoyable.

How is skin diving different from snorkeling?

Skin diving is swimming underwater, while holding your breath, using mask, fins, and snorkel. It is also known as "free diving" or "breath-hold diving." We will use these terms interchangeably throughout this book. They all mean the same thing.

Skin diving does not involve the use of tanks of compressed air, and although some people might think that skin diving implies that you go diving while naked, this just isn't true! A skin diver can wear a bathing suit, a Lycra® dive "skin" worn primarily for protection from the sun as well as cuts and scrapes, or a rubber wetsuit. Any of these garments could be worn and you would still be considered a "skin diver."

To be effective at skin diving, you need to be in good physical condition. You don't need to be a top athlete, but you do need to have a moderate level of fitness. Your ability to hold your breath underwater is greatly influenced by your physical condition.

Although instruction is not required for skin diving, it is strongly recommended. You must understand and be able to perform some basic skills, such as equalizing the pressure in your ears, which are essential to your health and safety if you want to descend even a few feet. By learning to equalize properly, you will be able to dive deeper underwater.

Skin diving is swimming underwater, with mask, fins, and snorkel, while holding your breath. No air tanks are worn for skin diving.

The ability to equalize the pressure in your ears will help you to avoid injury and accidents underwater. This book will help teach you how to equalize this pressure in the chapter on skin diving.

You must understand the risks of skin diving, which include the danger of underwater blackout, which kills a small number of competitive free divers every year. With proper training and knowledge, these risks are easy to avoid. This book will help teach you how to maximize your breath holding time underwater while minimizing the risk of underwater blackout.

Your ability to participate in skin diving is limited only by your capacity to hold your breath and the depth to which you can dive. With a minimum of practice, most people can easily free dive down to a depth of 20-30 feet underwater. Experienced free divers can regularly dive to depths between 60 and 100 feet. Truly exceptional free divers can attain depths in excess of 100 feet, but this requires dedication and practice.

Your ability to skin dive is limited by the amount of time you can hold your breath and the depth to which you can dive. Easy techniques to improve these skills are explained in this book.

It isn't necessary to dive deep to thoroughly enjoy skin diving. Most of the things that you will want to see while underwater are in depths shallower than 50 feet. The best light for underwater photography is in the first 30 feet of depth. Most marine life is also concentrated in shallower depths, where the sun penetrates the water more effectively. Skin diving is usually more expensive than snorkeling. Most serious skin divers will end up buying a wetsuit, weight belt, and other diving accessories. While these are not essential items, they will allow you to do more things underwater.

What is scuba diving?

Scuba is a word known as an "acronym," which means that each of the letters of the word stand for another separate word. Scuba stands for "self-contained underwater breathing apparatus," although the word has passed into common usage and the average person just assumes it means diving with compressed air tanks.

To participate in scuba diving you must be in good physical condition with no serious physical ailments, such as insulin dependent diabetes or medication dependent asthma. Scuba diving can be more strenuous than snorkeling or skin diving, because you must carry heavy scuba tanks and weights. Swimming with scuba gear takes more energy because the equipment is bulky and creates drag, slowing your movements in the water.

Instruction is essential to participate in scuba diving. Without instruction, you can injure or even kill yourself in a swimming pool using scuba equipment. It's not that scuba diving is particularly dangerous, but without knowledge and understanding of how the equipment works and the effects of breathing compressed air, you can injure yourself by an act as simple as holding your breath and surfacing in water depths as shallow as four feet.

The big advantage of scuba diving over skin diving is that with scuba equipment most people can dive deeper than they can while holding their breath. Obviously, you can also stay underwater much longer when you are carrying your air supply with you. This makes it easier to perform activities such as taking pictures underwater.

However, even scuba diving has its limitations and each individual diver is limited by his training, skill level, and experience. More experienced divers with the proper training can dive under more demanding conditions than less experienced divers.

Scuba diving is swimming underwater while using a "tank" usually filled with compressed air, which is used for breathing. Not everyone can participate in scuba diving.

Participating in scuba diving is more expensive than snorkeling or skin diving. To engage in scuba diving, at a minimum, you will need a wetsuit, weight belt, tank of compressed air, buoyancy compensator, regulator, submersible pressure gauge, and dive computer. Of course, this equipment can be rented, but rental costs add up over time and there is no substitute for the comfort and security of your own equipment.

It takes more time to clean up scuba equipment after a day of diving than it does snorkeling or skin diving gear, simply because there is more equipment and it is more complex. The equipment must also be inspected and serviced by an authorized repair facility on an annual basis.

Diving is a highly personal decision

No matter what form of diving you enjoy, whether it's snorkeling, skin diving, or scuba, it should be your decision alone whether or not you choose to participate in the sport. You should dive only because you want to do it, not because your spouse, parents, or children enjoy it.

You can experience the magic of snorkeling and diving almost anywhere there is water. With the simple skills explained in this book, you'll be able to start to explore the fascinating waters of our planet.

CHAPTER 2

EQUIPMENT FOR SNORKELING AND SKIN DIVING

Both snorkeling and skin diving require a certain amount of equipment for you to venture into the water comfortably. Some of the gear is considered "basic" and essential to participate in the sport. Other items are considered "accessories;" although for diving in cold water, you may feel that a wetsuit is essential, and you would be right!

Most diving instructors agree that the basic gear required to view sights from the surface and/or explore underwater would include the following items:

- Mask
- Fins
- Snorkel
- Some form of surface flotation assistance
- Diving partner or "buddy"

If you select quality gear for snorkeling, this equipment can almost always be used for skin or scuba diving as well. Buy good quality equipment and it will last you for many years.

Picking the right mask

Diving masks allow you to see underwater by placing a layer of air between your eyes and the water. Masks for snorkeling and skin diving are designed to cover your nose and eyes, but not your mouth.

Like most diving gear today, masks come in a wide range of styles, colors, and sizes. Almost any mask purchased from a quality sporting goods store or specialty dive shop will be acceptable provided it has a tempered glass lens and fits your face comfortably.

Masks come in a wide variety of shapes, colors, and sizes. Only a few types are shown here.

The fit of the mask is determined by the rubber seal that sits against your face. Generally, the softer the seal, the more comfortable the mask. However, no matter how comfortable the seal feels on your face, it will be ineffective if it allows water past the edge of the seal and into the mask.

To test the fit of the mask, fold the strap down over the front of the lens and hold the mask against your face. Make sure none of your hair is trapped underneath the seal. Inhale sharply through your nose and hold your breath. The mask should stay in position without the strap or you holding it in place.

The mask must fit your face properly. To test the fit, hold the mask against your face without using the strap and inhale. The mask should seal against your face and not fall off.

If the mask quickly falls away from your face, it does not fit. No matter how comfortable the mask feels, how much you like the color or design, if it doesn't make an effective seal against your face, don't buy it. You should never buy a mask unless you have the opportunity to try it on first, unless you are replacing an existing mask with the identical model.

There are masks with single lenses, dual lenses, and even as many as five lenses. You will find that smaller masks have a lower internal volume, weigh less, and are usually preferred for serious skin diving. Masks with more windows and higher volumes often have better visibility and are preferred by some divers for snorkeling and scuba diving.

Never buy a mask with a plastic lens because the lens will scratch and the optical quality will usually be poor. All quality diving masks are made from "tempered glass" and it will usually say this right on the lens, in fine print, up near the top of the glass. If it doesn't say "Tempered" or "Tempered Glass" on the lens, ask the salesperson. If they don't know, either select another mask or find someone who can confirm what type of lens has been used.

New masks must be prepared for use by washing them with a mild soap to remove any chemicals that remain from the manufacturing process. If this is not done the mask will "fog."

All new masks need to be prepared before using them for the first time by washing them with a mild dish soap to remove any chemicals that remain on the lens from the manufacturing process. Failure to remove these chemicals, which are not visible to your eye, will cause the mask to "fog" when you use it in the water, making it difficult to see clearly underwater.

If you wear contact lenses you can usually use them for diving, although you should check with your eye doctor to see if there are any special precautions you should take with the type you are wearing. If you wear glasses, prescription lenses are available for many different types of masks. Common prescriptions, for people who have no astigmatism and do not need especially thick lenses, are frequently available in stock at dive stores. Custom lenses can be ground to your exact prescription by several different companies in the U.S. Check with a local dive store for this service.

Goggles are not worn for snorkeling and especially for any type of diving where you descend below the surface. There are two problems with goggles. First, the lenses are not in the same plane, which causes distorted vision underwater. More importantly, since goggles do not cover your nose, when you use goggles underwater there is no way to equalize the pressure on the outside of them with the air space inside. This greater external pressure can cause serious injury to your eyes.

Goggles are not used for snorkeling or any type of diving.

With a mask, you can exhale a small amount of air from your nose into the mask so that the pressure inside equals the surrounding water pressure. This is impossible if you make the mistake of using goggles underwater. Never use goggles for any type of diving.

Snorkels are for breathing on the surface

Snorkels are "J" shaped tubes that are designed to allow you to breathe while resting on the surface without the need to lift your head each time you want to take a breath. With a snorkel, swimming on the surface is very easy in most situations.

Ideally, a snorkel should have a gentle curve to it, with no sharp bends or obstructions inside the breathing tube. The snorkel should be a maximum of 17 inches in length and have an internal diameter of one inch or more.

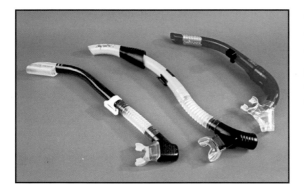

Snorkels should be as short as possible and have a gentle curved shape.

During surface swimming, it is inevitable for small amounts of water to occasionally enter the top of the snorkel. To prevent this water from reaching your mouth, better snorkels are equipped with some type of valve mechanism to help water drain out of the snorkel before this happens. However, if the snorkel is completely submerged it will fill up with water and this water must be cleared out of the snorkel before you can take another breath through it. This is a skill you will learn about later in this book.

Never buy a snorkel with a ping pong ball on the end of it!

In the past, cheap snorkels were equipped with a ping pong ball mechanism fitted to the top of the snorkel to prevent water from entering the snorkel if the diver went underwater. This type of mechanism never really worked and should not be used. Although there are modern snorkels that have more sophisticated valves that are designed to prevent water from entering the snorkel when you are submerged, these designs are not recommended since they typically make breathing more difficult.

The snorkel should have a comfortable mouthpiece that does not irritate your mouth. It must rest comfortably against the side of your head.

The snorkel must be attached to the mask with some type of "snorkel keeper" which is normally supplied with the snorkel when you buy it. Some snorkel keepers are made from rubber while others are made from plastic. You'll learn how to attach the snorkel to the mask in the chapter on snorkeling techniques.

Fins help you swim more efficiently

There are two main types of fins that are commonly used today; open heel adjustable fins and full foot fins. Both kinds are acceptable for snorkeling and diving. You may also hear people refer to fins as "flippers." Either term is acceptable.

Full foot fins are the most popular type of fins for snorkeling and skin diving in warmer waters. As their name implies, they usually cover the entire foot, except for an

Full foot fins are popular for snorkeling in warmer waters.

opening for the toes. They are usually light weight, relatively small, and inexpensive. They are a good choice for the casual diver.

If you want to use full foot fins in colder waters you will need to wear a pair of neoprene booties to keep your feet warm. Booties are like neoprene socks or boots that not only provide warmth, but also help protect your feet from rocks and other sharp objects.

You must purchase your booties when you purchase your fins in order to get the correct fit. Fins that fit with booties will not usually fit if you don't wear the booties. Conversely, fins that fit without booties won't usually fit if you try to wear booties with them.

Booties are a nice accessory whether you dive in warm or cold water. Low top booties are available specifically for warm water diving, although high top booties can be worn in warm or cold water.

Booties help keep your feet warm and help protect them from chafing. This pair is designed for cold water snorkeling and diving.

One drawback to full foot fins is that when the foot pocket on the fin wears out the fins cannot be repaired and must be thrown away. This is one of the reasons that more serious divers tend to use adjustable heel strap fins which have a longer useful life.

Thinner, low-top booties are used with open heel adjustable fins for diving in the tropics.

Open heel adjustable fins all have a replaceable heel strap.

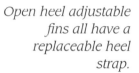

Open heel adjustable fins are designed with a removable strap which can be tightened or loosened to fit a wide range of foot sizes. These fins tend to be larger and heavier than full foot fins. This style of fins must usually be worn with a pair of booties to prevent blisters and chafing.

With open heel adjustable fins, the strap can be replaced when it wears out and the fins can be used for many years. This style of fin is preferred by avid skin and scuba divers because they generally provide better propulsion through the water.

Gloves help protect your hands

Gloves are very helpful in protecting your hands from cuts and scrapes, and to keep them warm in colder waters. There are many different styles of diving gloves made from cotton, plastic, neoprene, and other artificial materials.

While you can wear inexpensive cotton gardening gloves for snorkeling in warmer waters, they usually don't

Gloves will help protect your hands from cuts and scrapes in warm water.

hold up as well as gloves that are made especially for snorkeling and diving. Tropical diving gloves are usually made from a synthetic material that resists salt water and sun, with a palm that is made from a more rugged material.

Cold water diving gloves are usually made from foam neoprene, the same material used to make booties, diving hoods, and wet suits. This material provides good insulation for snorkeling and skin diving.

Surface flotation provides a place to rest

Whenever you go in the water it is recommended that you have some type of surface flotation available so that you have a place to rest if you become tired. Your surface flotation can be something as simple as an inner tube or a boogie board, or as sophisticated as a yacht. It doesn't matter what it is as long as you have some place to rest, especially if you are a long way from shore.

Personal flotation is a good idea

Although it is not considered essential, a personal flotation device is an excellent piece of accessory gear for snorkeling, especially if you are in water that is deep enough that you can't stand on the bottom. The personal flotation device is an inflatable vest that you wear to help increase your buoyancy to make it easier to rest while you are in the water. It's like having your own private island.

A snorkeling vest can help you rest on the surface.

The snorkeling vest holds a small amount of air, enough to make you slightly buoyant on the surface. It is equipped with a small tube with a valve that is used to inflate the vest with air from your lungs.

The buoyancy compensator is an inflatable vest that holds a much larger volume of air than the snorkeling vest. It can be used for scuba diving, although the most popular designs used for scuba diving today are somewhat different. With a buoyancy compensator, it is easier to make buoyancy adjustments if you are swimming with a heavy object, like a bag full of lobsters.

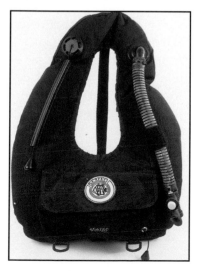

Some snorkeling vests and buoyancy compensators are equipped with CO_2 mechanisms which are supposed to provide instant buoyancy in the event of an emergency. These mechanisms must never be relied upon since

Buoyancy compensators hold more air and have more buoyancy than snorkeling vests.

they almost always rust and fail. If you have a choice of purchasing a snorkeling vest with or without a CO_2 cartridge inflator, save some money and get the one without it.

Both buoyancy compensators and snorkeling vests can be punctured by sharp objects. They can also be cut or damaged through careless use. When this happens they cannot be relied on to provide buoyancy as they normally would.

Neither the snorkeling vest nor the buoyancy compensator were designed as lifesaving devices. They must not be relied upon to save your life in the event of a cramp or exhaustion.

Everyone needs a buddy

Whenever you go in the water to enjoy snorkeling or skin diving, it is essential to always swim with a buddy or partner. They can provide you with assistance with your gear and may be able to help you in the event of an emergency.

A buddy can be a model for your underwater photos and can hold your equipment while you climb back aboard a

boat. With a buddy, you can share exciting moments and your buddy is someone to back up your stories when your other friends don't believe your tales of underwater adventure!

Keep in mind that for a buddy to be able to help you in an emergency they must have snorkeling and

It's always a good idea to have a buddy along whenever you go snorkeling.

diving skills at least equal to your own. If you are skin diving and pass out at depth, your buddy cannot assist you if he cannot dive to the same depths you can reach.

The concept of the buddy system is that both snorkelers or divers stay close together while in the water so that they can lend immediate assistance to each other. Ideally, you should be within touching distance of each other while on the surface in order to help one another quickly. While skin diving, it is recommended that one buddy always remains on the surface while the other dives.

You might think that if one buddy is good, two must be better, but this simply isn't true. In diving, three man buddy teams or large groups of divers acting as a buddy "team", simply aren't good ideas. In these situations, it's easy to lose track of each other, especially when one person thinks the other is watching the third buddy.

Everyone who participates in water sports, whether snorkeling, boating, or kayaking, should take a lifesaving course and have training in CPR and first aid.

In a large group it's easy for divers to lose track of their buddy.

Dive suits provide warmth and sun protection

For snorkeling in warm waters, a dive suit is normally not essential, but you may be more comfortable wearing a Lycra® dive "skin." A dive "skin" is a very thin, form fitting suit that provides protection from the sun, stinging sea creatures (which are rare in most places), and minor scrapes.

Dive skins provide protection from the sun as well as minor scrapes.

Dive skins are stylish and ideal for tropical diving. They are available in an incredible array of colors. Unlike a wetsuit, however, dive skins provide no buoyancy.

In cooler waters, or if you plan to spend lots of time in warm water, you may prefer to use a very thin wetsuit. Wetsuits are made from a synthetic rubber known as foam neoprene. There are thousands of tiny nitrogen bubbles in this material which provide insulation and give the suit a great deal of buoyancy. If you wear a wetsuit and you only plan to snorkel, without diving underwater, you'll find the wetsuit makes floating effortless.

Thin tropical wetsuits are usually no more than two or three millimeters (1/8 inch) thick. You can purchase "shorty" suits, with short sleeves and legs, or one-piece full coverage suits that protect your entire body. These suits are ideal for skin diving and scuba diving in tropical waters, above 75°F. They are thin and flexible, yet provide reasonable insulation.

Thin tropical wetsuits are ideal for long exposures in warmer waters.

For waters between 68 and 75°F, most people will be comfortable with a 3/16 inch (3-4 mm) thick wetsuit. The suit should include both jacket and pants; a hood may not be necessary.

For colder waters, below 68°F, a thick wetsuit is normally worn. The rubber used to make these

suits is usually about six to seven millimeters (1/4 inch) thick. There are numerous different styles of suits, but the most popular ones usually consist of a "farmer-john" set of bib overalls, and a separate jacket with an attached hood. These suits have tremendous buoyancy.

In cold water, a thicker wetsuit is usually required.

Keep in mind that each person varies in how much insulation they need to be comfortable in the water. Smaller, thinner divers usually need to wear a thicker wetsuit with more coverage than larger, heavier divers. No matter what type of suit your dive partner wears, you need to wear a suit that provides enough insulation for your personal needs.

The most popular wetsuits have nylon on both the inside and outside of the suit. The nylon on the inside makes it easier to don the suit. The nylon on the outside makes the suit more resistant to abrasion and can be ordered in a variety of colors.

A wetsuit must fit snugly to be effective. The suit allows a small amount of water to enter the openings at the wrist, ankles, neck, and waist. This water is warmed to your body's temperature, and in combination with the suit's own insulation, helps to keep you warm.

While some people find that they can wear an "off-the-rack" wetsuit, many people find they need a custom suit to get the best fit. Any good sport diving store should be able to help you determine whether you can wear a "stock" suit or need one customized to your measurements.

Wetsuits can be ordered with a variety of special features including pockets, knife sheaths, knee pads, and "spine pads" to help fill the void along the small of your back. How many options you get on your suit is a personal decision dependent on your needs and the size of your wallet!

Wear a hood to prevent body heat loss through your head in colder waters.

If the water is cold enough to wear a thick wetsuit, you'll almost certainly want to wear a hood, too. Much of your body's heat is lost through your head, so a properly fitting hood can go a long way toward making diving more enjoyable. You can either buy a separate hood or get a jacket with a hood attached to it, as mentioned previously. In colder waters, an attached hood will provide the most warmth.

Weight belts allow you to adjust your buoyancy

Most people find that they float rather easily in salt water while swimming. To make it easier to submerge, many divers wear a few pounds of lead weight on a weight belt. The exact amount of weight needed is different for each person, but in this book you'll learn how to check your buoyancy and add just enough weight to make diving easy. Chapter 5 explains how to check your buoyancy properly.

Skin divers who wear wetsuits must wear enough weight to neutralize the buoyancy of the suit for diving. The thicker the wetsuit, the more weight you will need to dive.

There are several different types of weights and weight belts that are commonly used. Molded weights are designed to be used with weight belts made from nylon webbing. These weights may be bare lead or they may be coated with plastic. Larger molded weights are usually curved to fit your body and are called "hip weights."

Plastic-covered molded weights are available in many colors. Note the colored weight keepers used to prevent the weights from sliding on the weight belt.

Bags of lead shot are also available in different sizes that are specifically designed for diving. The bags are designed to be used in belts equipped with pouches to hold them. Smaller divers and divers with prominent hip bones usually find shot belts to be more comfortable than belts with molded weights.

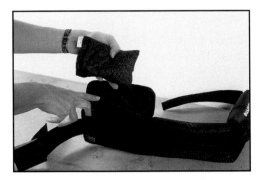

Shot filled bags are used in belts with pouches.

No matter what type of belt you select, the one feature that is common to all weight belts is the quick release buckle. This is an essential safety item. The quick release is designed to open easily with one hand in the event of an emergency. If you become exhausted or feel like you are going to pass out while you are in the water it is essential to drop your weight belt.

Special weight belt buckles are also available that are spring loaded to allow the belt to be tightened and compensate for the compression of your dive suit while you are underwater. They are a big help in preventing the belt from rotating on your body.

To assemble a belt using molded weights, you'll need to pick up some plastic weight keepers to help keep the weights from sliding around on the belt. One keeper goes on either side of each weight.

The belt should be trimmed to the correct size for you, but this must be done while you are wearing your dive suit. If you trim the belt when you aren't wearing your suit, it will probably be too short. Once the belt is trimmed, the end of

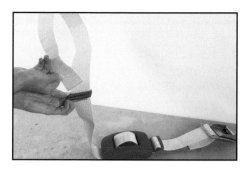

Plastic weight keepers will keep your weights from sliding on your belt.

Trim the belt to the correct length. Be sure to check this with the belt loaded with weights and while you are wearing your dive suit.

the belt should be singed with a match to prevent the nylon from unraveling. Take care not to touch the hot nylon because it will stick to your skin and cause a serious burn.

Always fly a dive flag

Whenever you go snorkeling, be sure to fly a diver's down flag from your boat or surface float. This is essential to help avoid getting hit by a careless boat operator.

The diver's flag is a red flag with a diagonal white stripe which runs from the upper left corner to the lower right. The purpose of the flag is to warn boat operators that there are divers in the water and that they should maintain a distance of 100 feet from the flag. If you venture more than 100 feet in any direction from your flag you run a good chance of being hit by a boat.

Keep in mind that not all yachtsmen know what the diver's flag means and that some people will deliberately motor your way to investigate your flag! Keep a sharp eye out any time you are snorkeling in an area where there is any boat traffic.

Always fly a diver's down flag from your boat or surface float.

Marking your equipment

If you plan to use your equipment at resorts where there are other divers present, you will probably want to mark your gear so that you can quickly identify it as yours. You can use a waterproof marking pen for this purpose on brightly colored gear. Dive stores also sell special markers designed for use on dark equipment.

Never wear earplugs underwater!

While it is acceptable to wear earplugs for swimming and snorkeling on the surface, you must never wear earplugs for diving below the surface.

Never wear earplugs if you plan to dive below the surface.

The water pressure can drive the earplugs through your eardrums causing serious injury.

Maintaining your dive gear

Good quality diving equipment will last you for many years, but only if you care for it properly. There are a few simple things you need to know to get the most out of your gear.

- Always rinse your diving equipment thoroughly with fresh water at the end of each diving day. If you allow salt to dry on your gear it can cause it to wear prematurely.

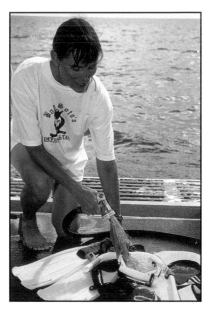

Be sure to rinse your equipment thoroughly with fresh clean water after each day of snorkeling.

- If you use a snorkeling vest or buoyancy compensator, each time you put air into the vest or vent it while you are in the water some salt water will get inside. You need to run fresh water into the vest to help flush it clean. To flush your buoyancy device, hold the inflator mechanism open and squirt fresh water into it.

• Shake the vest several times and turn it over so that the fresh water circulates inside it completely. Turn the device upside down and hold it so the valve is at the lowest point. Open the valve and allow the water to drain out. Repeat this process until the water flowing out of the vest appears to be clear.

Flush the inside of your snorkeling vest with fresh water.

Drain all the water out of your snorkeling vest prior to storage.

- Dry your gear in the shade where it will get good air circulation. Never leave your gear in the sun any longer than necessary.
- Hang your wetsuit or dive skin on a wide wetsuit hanger (available at most dive stores) to dry and for storage. Wetsuits in particular should not be folded for storage or they will develop permanent creases.
- Store your gear in a cool, dry place between diving days. Keep it away from electric motors or hot water heaters which produce ozone and cause rubber products to deteriorate.

Hang your wetsuit on a wide hanger to dry it. It should also be hung for storage.

CHAPTER 3

ACCESSORIES FOR SNORKELING AND SKIN DIVING

There are many accessories that divers use to extend their abilities and make diving more fun. Some items, like a gear bag, make things more convenient. Other gadgets, like a dive light, will help you to explore shipwrecks and look into holes in the reef to see the marine life hiding there.

Dive knives are tools

Dive knives are not used as weapons for fighting off marine life. A dive knife can be a very important tool, especially if you are diving in an area where there are fishing lines, nets, or thick aquatic weeds. If you get involved in spearfishing, you'll find that a dive knife is essential.

Dive knives come with either a sharp or blunt tip. A blunt tip is recommended to help avoid the possibility of stabbing yourself! If you're a spearfisherman, you should purchase a knife with a sharp tip, which is used to help clean fish or kill a wounded fish.

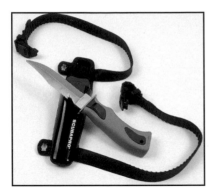

A dive knife is a tool, not a weapon.

Most knives have a serrated edge on one side and a razor edge on the other. The serrated edge is good for cutting line, which is the most common application for the knife.

Every dive knife is supplied with a sheath, which can usually be mounted on your weight belt or the inside of your leg. Most people find that mounting the sheath on the inside of the leg is more convenient, since they can see the sheath in that location when they are wearing a mask.

To keep your dive knife in good condition, be sure to rinse it after each day of diving, dry it, and apply a light coat of oil or other corrosion inhibitor, such as WD40®.

Get attention with a whistle

A waterproof whistle is an important accessory any time you snorkel or dive in a remote location, especially if you are far from shore. The whistle will let you signal for help at much further distances than you can effectively shout. Most dive stores and marine hardware stores sell this type of whistle.

Dive lights are useful during the daytime, too

Although you might think that a dive light would only be useful at night, a light can be a handy accessory during the day. Lights are especially useful around shipwrecks and for checking out shy marine creatures that hide in crevices in the reef.

If you develop your skin diving skills to the point where you can dive to depths in excess of 30 feet, a light will allow you to see the colors which are filtered out by the water as you dive deeper. In deep water, colors appear drab and dull, but with a light, the colors of the depths appear vibrant, with many reds, oranges, and yellows.

Many people go snorkeling or skin diving at night. During the evening hours, you will often see fish and other critters who are hidden during the daytime. Lobsters, who live in holes during the day, come out and walk the bottom at night, making them much easier to catch.

Dive lights vary in strength and size, but you don't usually need a large light. There are many small lights that are quite powerful. Smaller lights tend to be less expensive and aren't as heavy.

Dive lights must be both pressure proof and water-proof. A waterproof light used for boating is inadequate for snorkeling or skin diving. Even if you hold the light just a few feet under the surface, the additional pressure will cause most lights that are merely "waterproof" to leak.

Dive lights are useful even during the day, especially for looking into holes in the reef.

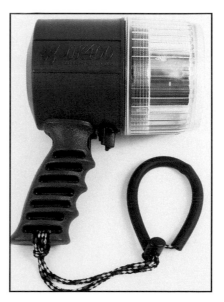

Dive lights, like underwater cameras, use round rubber "o-rings" to seal out water and pres-sure. O-rings must be in their proper position, clean, and lubricated with a light coating of o-ring grease in order to work properly. If you buy a dive light, be sure to ask the dive store salesman to show you how to check and lubricate the o-ring.

Your dive light should be equipped with a lanyard to help prevent you from losing it. For snorkeling and skin diving, you'll probably want a dive light that floats. However, for scuba diving, most divers prefer a light that sinks, so they can set the light down if they need to while working on the bottom.

A gear bag will keep you organized

You will find it much easier to transport your equipment to and from the dive site if you have a gear bag for carrying your equipment. This becomes more important the more gear you own and use.

Some gear bags have multiple pockets which can be very handy if you carry lots of small accessory items. Others are divided into wet and dry compartments, which work well, particularly if you are using a dive suit or carrying extra clothing.

For tropical diving, a mesh gear bag is often a good idea because it will allow air to circulate through the bag, helping the gear to dry and discouraging the formation of mold and mildew. You will also find that if the bag isn't too full, you can dunk the entire bag in the rinse trough used by most dive resorts to rinse your gear.

One piece of gear that doesn't go in your dive bag is your weight belt.

Keep your gear together by using a gear bag. Bags are available in many sizes.

The belt will make your bag too heavy and can damage the seams of the bag and the fabric itself. Carry your belt separately.

A bag for your underwater treasures

Goody bags are simple mesh bags which are useful for carrying any "treasures" you may collect while you are underwater, such as shells, lobsters, old bottles, or similar items. The bags come in different sizes. If you have a small amount of gear, your goody bag can double as your gear bag.

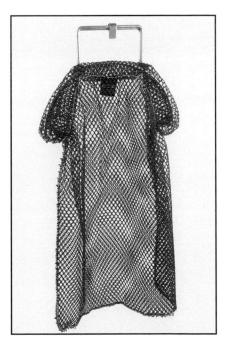

Mesh bags like this goody bag are useful for carrying any "treasure" you may collect while snorkeling. If you don't have much gear, a goody bag can double as your gear bag.

CHAPTER 4

SNORKELING TECHNIQUES

The basic techniques of snorkeling are skills that apply to all diving. Donning and removing your gear properly, snorkel breathing, and swimming with fins can easily be mastered by anyone who enjoys swimming. Almost anyone can learn these skills in under an hour.

Assembling the mask and snorkel

Before you can enter the water, you'll need to assemble your mask and snorkel. Different manufacturers use various types of snorkel keepers to attach the snorkel to the mask, but the snorkel is usually attached to the left side of the mask. The reason behind this is that for scuba diving, the regulator comes over the right shoulder.

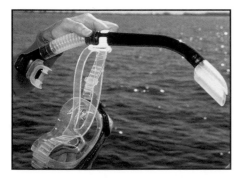

There are many types of clips and "keepers" used to attach snorkels to masks. Most of the better designs today allow the snorkel to be detached from the mask for travel.

Bringing the snorkel over the left side helps prevent confusion that would result if the snorkel and regulator were routed over the same shoulder. If you think you may want to try scuba some day, get in the habit of using the snorkel on the left. If you have no intention of ever scuba diving, you can put your snorkel on whichever side you prefer.

Once your snorkel and mask are assembled, put them aside while you don your other gear. The snorkel and mask are normally the last gear you will put on before entering the water.

Donning the dive skin

If you plan to use a dive suit, it's usually easiest if you sit down to don the suit. This is especially important if you will be snorkeling from a boat. If you try to stand up while you pull the bottom of the suit on, you may fall and injure yourself or other people around you. Always sit down while donning the bottom part of your suit.

Donning a dive skin is very simple. The slick Lycra® surface will slide easily over your skin and the material has

tremendous stretch. Open the zipper on the suit all the way and slide your feet into the legs and position the "stirrups" over the soles of your feet. Pull the suit up along your legs as far as it will go and then stand up.

Once the suit is up to your torso, insert your arms into the sleeves one arm at a time, and pull the rest of the suit up onto your shoulders. If the suit has a front

Sit down to don your dive skin.

Insert one leg at a time into the wetsuit pants and pull the suit over your feet.

zip, you'll be able to close it yourself. If it has a back zip, you'll need your dive buddy to close it for you.

Donning a wetsuit

Donning a wetsuit is similar to donning a dive skin, except that wetsuits are generally thicker and do not have as much stretch. The thicker the suit, the more time it will take to put it on.

To don the suit, first make sure you have the suit oriented properly. There is a back and a front to all wetsuits. Look at the curve of the legs and the bend of the arms to help figure out which is the front and which is the back. On a woman's suit, the jacket will be cut with darts for her breasts.

Work the suit up your body by grabbing a fold of material and working it up a few inches at a time.

Sit down and insert your legs into the suit and pull the suit over your feet. You'll need to pull the bottom of the suit up a bit at a time, starting at your thighs and working it up your body.

Grab a small fold of the suit between your thumb and forefinger and work the material up a few inches. This action will need to be repeated several times, especially with thicker suits. Work the pants up until they are all the way up to your crotch. If your wetsuit pants hang too low below your crotch you won't be able to kick effectively, and you'll look pretty funny, too, somewhat like a child whose diaper is dragging.

Once the suit is up to your hips, stand up so that you can pull it all the way up and insert your arms in the sleeves.

If the pants are the farmer-john style, slip the top over your shoulders. Some farmer-johns have Velcro® closures at the shoulders.

Once you've donned your pants you'll want to don your booties. Simply unzip the zipper and pull them onto your feet as you would a pair of socks. Booties have a left and right, so be sure you have the correct bootie on the correct foot. Roll the top of the wetsuit pants at the ankle over the top of the booties so the booties are covered by the ankles of the wetsuit. This will help streamline you in the water and make swimming easier, otherwise the booties tend to balloon up with water.

If your suit has a separate jacket, with full length sleeves, insert one arm into a sleeve at a time and work it on all the way

Roll the top of your wetsuit pants over the top of your booties.

before slipping into the other arm. With thicker suits, if you grab the cuff and pull it away from the inside of your wrist, you can blow air from your mouth up the sleeve to help the sleeve slide into position. You can do this yourself, or if you and your buddy are really good friends, he can do it for you. It works better if your arm is extended and someone else blows the air up the sleeve. Don't laugh until you've tried it!

Most wetsuit jackets either have a "beaver tail" that must be fastened to hold the jacket down, or a "step-in" design for the jacket. If your jacket is equipped with a beaver-tail be sure it is fastened or the suit will ride up on your body while you are in the water.

Slide one arm into your jacket at a time.

Be sure to fasten the beaver tail on your wetsuit jacket.

Your hood should be tucked underneath the shoulders of your jacket. Pull the hood over your head and have your buddy tuck it in for you. Some jackets have attached hoods, which can be left down until you are ready to enter the water.

If the weather is warm topside, you may want to jump into the water to get wet before donning the rest of your gear, to help avoid overheating.

Adjusting the snorkeling vest

When you are using a snorkeling vest, it should be donned immediately after you don your wetsuit. All vests have a waist strap and some also have a crotch strap, which helps to keep the vest from riding up on your body. Open both straps before you slide the vest over your head.

The crotch strap on the snorkeling vest must be adjusted to the right length.

SNORKELING FUN

Once the vest is positioned around your neck, you'll need to adjust the straps. The straps should be adjusted so that there is enough space for you to put a closed fist between your chest and the vest itself. This will allow you to breathe deeply without restriction. If there isn't enough space for your fist, you must loosen the straps.

The waist belt should be adjusted so it is snug but you can breathe comfortably.

Donning fins

The easiest way don a full foot fin is to sit down, wet the inside of the fin, if possible, grasp it firmly by both sides of the blade, and pull it onto your foot. Once your toes are all the way into the fin, you can reach back and slide the heel of the fin onto your foot.

You can don your fins while standing up on a beach, but you'll need to lean on your buddy to do this without falling. In addition, since you'll be using one hand to lean on your partner, it will be a bit more difficult to don your fins, particularly if they are snug.

The technique for donning adjustable heel strap fins is very similar except that you must loosen the straps before donning the fins. If you're sitting, hold the fin with both hands and slide it on, then position the heel strap and tighten it until snug.

To don a full foot fin, grasp the fin by both sides and pull it onto your foot.

Put one finger inside the heel pocket of the fin and slide it over your heel.

On an adjustable heel strap fin, be sure the strap is snug but not tight.

If you're standing up, you can either hold the fin and slide it on or put it down, stand on the blade with your other foot, and thrust your foot into the foot pocket. Once the fin is on the front of your foot, position the heel strap and tighten it.

Last minute mask preparation

Just prior to entering the water and donning your mask, you'll want to "prepare" the mask so that the inside of the lens doesn't "fog" while you're in the water. If this is not done, water droplets will form on the inside of the lens and make it difficult to see.

There are several different ways to prepare the mask and they all work well. The simplest method is somewhat disgusting, but it's cheap, simple, and almost always available. While the mask is still dry, simply spit onto the lens, swirl the saliva around, and dunk the mask briefly in the water to wash out the big "chunks." Your saliva will form a thin film on the lens which will help keep the mask from fogging. This sounds gross, but it works and it's how most divers handle this problem.

If you're diving in California where there is kelp, you can also use this seaweed to do the same thing. Other people use tobacco (which makes your mask smell like you're

diving in an ashtray) or even a potato. There are also commercially available mask "defog" solutions which you can buy at dive stores if you feel you must. However, the reality is that most people just use spit.

If you'd rather not spit in your mask to keep it from fogging up, commercial mask defoggers are available.

Donning your mask

To don the mask, position it on your face so that it is oriented properly and slide the strap down onto the back of your head. Make sure the strap is not twisted and not too low.

The mask should be snug on your face, but it should not be tight. If it is too loose, it will leak. If it is too tight, it will become uncomfortable very quickly. When you take your mask off and there is a red ring on your skin where the mask seal was located, the mask was too tight.

Hold the mask against your face as you slide the strap over your head.

Make sure all your hair is out of the mask before you seal it against your face.

When the mask strap is correctly positioned it should be fairly high up on the back of your head.

There must be no hair trapped under the seal of the mask or it will leak. If you're wearing a hood, the face seal for the mask goes underneath the hood and seals on your face, just as it would normally. If the face seal goes over the hood, the mask will leak.

Don't forget your gloves

Most divers put their gloves on either right before they put their mask on or right after. Be sure to fasten any tabs that help hold the gloves on your hand.

Rigging the dive flag

Always be sure to use a diver's down flag whenever you are snorkeling or skin diving. If you are diving from a small boat, be sure to hoist the flag right before you enter the water. If you are using a boogie board or inner tube, your flag should be rigged with a clamp or other attachment so it will stand vertically and can be seen easily by boat operators. Most dive stores sell devices to help rig your flag.

Breathing through the snorkel

Breathing through a snorkel takes a bit more effort than breathing normally. You must breathe just a bit more forcefully and deeply than you would without the snorkel. If you don't breathe strongly enough you will become exhausted very quickly.

When you are snorkeling on the surface, occasionally waves will lap over the top of your snorkel. If your snorkel is equipped with a top valve, this should help keep most of the water out of the mouthpiece. However, if the snorkel is completely submerged, it will fill with water.

You must learn to become attuned to what's known as the "snorkel tension," which is how easy it is to draw air through the snorkel. The moment this changes this is a signal that water has entered the snorkel. You must also learn to control your airway, so that if you are inhaling you know to instantly stop if you sense water entering the snorkel.

*As you rest or swim on the surface, you must breathe through
the snorkel a bit more deeply than your normally do.*

Snorkels not equipped with self-draining valves must
be cleared of water when they are flooded. The most effective way to do this is to use the "blast method" of snorkel
clearing. To do this, forcefully exhale whenever the snorkel
fills with water to blast the water out. Before you take another breath, it is important to inhale cautiously to ensure there
is no water left in the snorkel. By inhaling cautiously, you
can actually breathe "around" small amounts of water in the
snorkel. However, if you inhale vigorously, you will suck up
any remaining water in the snorkel.

If you have difficulty mastering the blast method of
snorkel clearing, you can always simply lift your head out of
the water, and remove the snorkel from your mouth. This
will allow the water to drain out of the snorkel. This method
is acceptable, although in this position it's more likely you
will swallow some water if any waves hit your face. It's also
not considered very professional and will mark you as a
novice snorkeler.

Clearing water from the snorkel by the blast method requires a forceful exhalation.

Proper fin kicks are important

In order to be a good snorkeler you must develop an effective kick. With most fins, you'll want to kick from the hip to get good propulsion. Other types of fins, such as the Force Fin®, which is very popular with snorkelers, work best when you kick with a bent knee.

When you are swimming on the surface, it's important to keep your fins in the water. If you are kicking your fins out of the water in the air, you will get no thrust from your fins.

You can swim face down, on your back, or on your side, depending on where you are going and how fast you want to get there. Swimming face down is usually fastest, but takes more energy and is usually the most fatiguing method. Swimming on your back or on your side is easier, but is usually not as fast as swimming face down. When you swim face down you should occasionally "bob" your head out of the water to check to see you're heading in the direction you intended to go.

In snorkeling or skin diving you need to get in the habit of only using your legs for propulsion and not using your arms. Your arms provide little propulsion compared to your

Your fins only provide propulsion when they are in the water. Don't let your feet break the surface when you are kicking.

You can swim on your back if you get tired, or for a change of pace, but you won't be able to use your snorkel when you do this.

You can swim on your side if you prefer.

legs when you are wearing fins. In addition, if you are carrying a camera or other gear you won't be able to use your arms.

If you swim on your back you won't be able to use your snorkel, and you may want to remove your mask so that you can breathe through your nose and mouth. In this situation, slide your mask down around your neck by pulling the front down, and let it hang there.

Swimming through aquatic plants

Whenever you swim through aquatic plants, such as kelp, you must move slowly and methodically. Although the plants may snag on your fins or snorkel, they will not wrap themselves around you and drag you to the bottom. It's a simple matter to just pull the fronds of the plant off of whatever piece of gear they have caught on.

To swim across thick kelp on the surface you must "kelp crawl." Pull yourself through the kelp by grabbing a handful at a time and pulling it towards you.

To swim across thick kelp on the surface you must use a technique known as "kelp crawling." With your face in the water as you lay horizontal on the surface, lift one arm and extend it ahead of you. Lower your hand into the water and grab as much kelp as you can and pull it towards your chest. Repeat the action with the other arm. You will be surprised at how quickly you can move through the water this way.

Never put your mask on your forehead

Never put your mask on your forehead unless you are willing to lose it or want to be rescued. When your mask is on your forehead there is a good chance that the next wave that comes along will knock it off your head and you will

Avoid putting your mask on your forehead unless you want to risk losing it.

If you must remove your mask while you are in the water, slide it down around your neck.

lose it. In addition, when snorkelers and divers are in distress, the first thing they usually will do is place the mask on their forehead.

Putting your mask on your forehead is like waving a red flag to any divemaster or lifeguard who happens to see you in this position. They will instantly assume you are in trouble and will usually enter the water immediately to come rescue you.

If you want to remove your mask while you are in the water, slide it down around your neck. This will help keep you from losing it.

How to signal to the boat or shore

Whether you snorkel from a boat or shore, there are usually people around to oversee your activity and help ensure your safety. On a charter snorkeling boat, there will frequently be a person designated as the "divemaster" who is there to ensure that everyone follows the proper safety procedures and has a good time. On the beach, there will often be a lifeguard.

As a snorkeler, the divemaster or lifeguard will sometimes signal to you at a distance to check to see if you are okay. There are two ways for them to signal to you and for you to respond properly. One technique is to take one of your arms and elevate it as high as possible to your side, out of the water, placing your hand on your head. This forms a large "O" for "okay!" This is both a question and an answer. If the divemaster gives you this signal, you should respond with the same signal, as long as you are okay.

Another method for signaling "okay" is to lift both your arms over your head, out of the water, and clasp your hands together, which also forms a big "O", indicating you are okay. Again, this is both a question and an answer.

To signal that you need help in the water, look at the boat or shore, lift your arm as high as it will go, and wave your closed fist. This is a sign that you need immediate

Signal that you are "okay" by forming an "O" over your head with both arms.

assistance. Of course, this signal only works if people are looking in your direction. If they are looking elsewhere, you will need to use your whistle to attract attention.

Never wave at people on the boat or on the beach, because this movement looks similar to the signal for help. It's embarrassing to have someone come rescue you if you don't really need it!

If you regularly snorkel in remote locations, you may want to

Another way to signal you're okay is with a single hand placed atop your head.

SNORKELING FUN

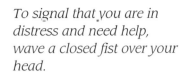

To signal that you are in distress and need help, wave a closed fist over your head.

Inflatable tubes like this are available for signaling to a boat at a distance.

purchase an inflatable tube that can be used as a signaling device. Dive shops sell these under various names, such as "Scuba Tuba" and "Safety Sausage."

Removing your fins

When you are diving from a boat you should never remove your fins unless you are holding onto some part of the boat, like the dive ladder. If you remove your fins and there is any current it will be very difficult to swim back to the boat.

To remove open heel adjustable fins, loosen the buckle or strap on one fin at a time and slide the strap over your heel. Pull the fin off your foot and hand it up onto the boat.

To remove full foot fins, slide one finger in the heel of the fin and pop it over your heel. Grab the side of the fin and pull it off your foot.

Removing your mask

Grasp both sides of the front of the mask and pull the mask away from your face until it just clears your nose. Lift the mask upwards and the strap will slide off your head.

Removing your dive suit

To remove a Lycra® dive skin, unzip the suit and peel it off your body. It will slide off very easily. Removing a thin tropical wetsuit is just as easy.

Removing a thicker wetsuit is a bit more difficult. First open all of the zippers on the suit. Next, unzip the jacket and peel it off.

If you have a jacket with an attached hood, unzip the jacket and flip the back of it up until you can grab the beaver tail on the suit. Lift the front edge of the hood up over your mouth. Bend over and pull the beaver tail towards your head until you can pull the folded back of the jacket over your head. Peel the arms down inside out.

To remove the pants, fold the top down and keep pulling the pants down your leg. The nylon will slide against itself. The most difficult part will be getting the cuffs of the pants over your feet.

CHAPTER 5

SKIN DIVING TECHNIQUES

This chapter includes the techniques you will use if you plan to dive below the surface while holding your breath. If you only intend to remain on the surface and never want to swim down for a closer look at things on the bottom, then you don't need to read this chapter. However, if you plan to hold your breath and dive any distance below the surface, this chapter is essential reading.

Never use earplugs for swimming underwater!

As a skin diver swimming underwater you must never wear earplugs while breath-hold diving. The problem with earplugs is that as the pressure increases as you dive deeper, the earplugs can actually rupture your eardrum and be forced into your ears. This will cause you to suffer from dizziness (vertigo) as water enters the middle ear and could result in drowning and death. At the very least, if your eardrum ruptures you may end up with an infection and you will probably suffer some hearing loss after the eardrum heals.

To prevent any damage caused by ear plugs while diving simply be sure to never wear ear plugs for swimming underwater.

Donning the weight belt

As a snorkeler, if you don't intend to go underwater, you don't need to wear a weight belt. To dive below the surface, as a skin diver, you may need to wear a small amount of weight, even if you aren't wearing a wetsuit.

Two things are essential when you are wearing a weight belt. First, your belt must always have a clear drop path, so that if you ditch it, it will fall cleanly away from your body. Secondly, you should always don your belt so that the buckle is oriented the same way. If you are right handed, you will probably want a right hand release, so that the buckle opens to the right. If you are left handed, you will probably prefer a left hand release, with the buckle opening to the left. It doesn't matter which way you set your belt up so long as you get in the habit of being consistent about the way you do it.

Your weight belt should always be the last piece of gear you don after your dive suit and snorkeling vest (or buoyancy compensator). Your belt must never be under your vest, especially if the vest is equipped with a crotch strap where the belt might hang up if you needed to drop it.

The easiest way to don the belt is to "step into it", by holding it low to the ground in front of you, and stepping over it one leg at a time. Lift the belt to your waist, lay it across your back at your waist, bend

Don the weight belt after the snorkeling vest. Step over the belt one leg at a time before raising it to your waist.

The weight belt must be clear of the straps of the snorkeling vest.

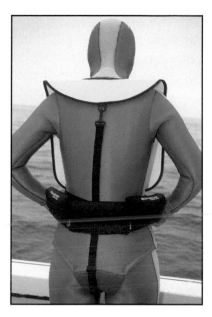

forward, and tighten the belt until it is snug. The buckle should be situated in the front of your body at waist level.

You will usually find that once you enter the water, the belt will tend to slide around a bit. It is important to check the buckle on the belt occasionally when you are in the water to make sure that it is oriented in the proper position. If the buckle has slid and it is behind you, you will not be able to locate it quickly should you need to drop the belt.

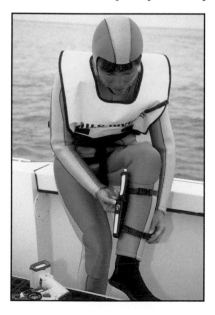

Your knife is usually easiest to find if it is on your leg

As a skin diver, it's always a good idea to carry a dive knife with you, and most people find it most convenient to mount the knife on the inside of their calf, on the leg opposite from the hand they use. If you are right handed, mount the knife on the

Your knife can be mounted on the inside of your calf.

inside of your left calf. If you're left handed, mount it on the inside of your right calf.

Be sure to adjust the straps on the knife so that they are snug, but not tight. Most straps are made from stretchy rubber and should have a bit of tension on them to hold the knife in position.

Checking your buoyancy

One of the most critical things you must do to be successful as a skin diver is to learn how to check and adjust your buoyancy. If you don't wear enough weight, you will be "positively buoyant" and find that it is difficult or impossible to dive underwater. You can't sink or dive if you are positively buoyant.

If you wear too much weight you will be "negatively buoyant" which will make it a struggle for you to swim and rest easily on the surface. This can be exhausting if you don't do something to correct the situation.

The personal buoyancy of your body, your dive suit, and all of the rest of your equipment will affect your buoyancy in the water. Ideally, you will want to be either "neutrally buoyant" or just slightly "positively buoyant."

The big question is, how much weight do you need? If you're wearing a thin, tropical wetsuit (1/8 inch thick neoprene), start with 4% of your body weight. If you weigh 165 pounds, you would start out by wearing six pounds of weight.

For divers wearing a full cold water wetsuit, made from 1/4 inch thick neoprene, start with 8% of your body weight. This may be a bit on the light side for some people, but it is better to be too light than too heavy.

To test your buoyancy, enter the water wearing all your equipment, in a location where you can reach out and touch the dive boat or surface float. Have extra weights available on the boat or shore to add to your belt if you need them, but always start your tests with the minimum amount of weight.

If you are properly weighted for skin diving, you should float at about eye level, or just a bit higher.

The water should be just deep enough so that your fins don't touch the bottom. With your snorkel in your mouth, and your body hanging vertically in the water, take a big deep breath, and relax. Don't kick or use your arms to maintain your position. See where you float.

If you float with your eyes right at the surface of the water, theoretically, you are perfectly weighted. If you start

to sink you are too heavily weighted and must remove some weight. Kick back to the surface, exit the water, and adjust your weights. If you float with your whole head out of the water, you are too light and should add weight a pound at a time and test again until you have exactly the right

If you float with your whole head out of the water, you are too buoyant to skin dive easily.

amount of weight. It is better to be just a bit "light" than to be too heavily weighted.

You can run the same buoyancy test even if you aren't wearing a wetsuit, but you probably won't need to wear more than four pounds of weight. However, some people are especially buoyant and may need more weight. Take your time and experiment. Just be sure to add only one pound of weight at a time.

Remember that any time that you add accessories they will change your buoyancy. For example, most underwater cameras, dive lights, and spear guns are negatively buoyant and will sink to the bottom on their own. When you carry these items while diving it's like carrying more weights.

It's also important to know that when you are wearing a wetsuit, as you dive deeper, the suit will compress and you will lose buoyancy. This will change your buoyancy underwater, even at a depth of 15 feet. If you dive deep enough, the compression of your suit and the resulting negative buoyancy can make it a real struggle to get back to the surface! In a situation like this, your only option may to be to drop your weight belt in order to get back to the top.

Never wear any more weight than you absolutely must to dive. Elsewhere in this chapter you will learn some effective techniques for surface diving that will allow you to overcome a slight amount of positive buoyancy from your wetsuit. This will allow you to float easily at the surface, yet you will be neutrally buoyant at depth as your suit compresses, which is considered the ideal way to breath-hold dive.

As your wetsuit is used it will gradually lose some of its buoyancy and over time, you will need to remove some of the weight from your belt. If you lose or gain a few pounds this will also affect your buoyancy. If you buy a new wetsuit its buoyancy will probably be different from the suit you owned previously. Check your buoyancy periodically to make sure it hasn't changed.

Equalizing the pressure in your ears

As you dive underwater, the deeper you go, the greater the pressure. In order to dive comfortably and avoid injury, it is essential to equalize the pressure in your ears. If you fail to do this, you can rupture your eardrum causing dizziness underwater. This can lead to drowning in extreme cases, or infections and loss of hearing in less serious instances.

Before you ever leave the surface, it is essential to start equalizing the pressure in your ears. Divers also refer to this as "clearing your ears." This can be done several ways, either by yawning or wiggling your jaws from side to side. You will probably find the most effective technique is to pinch your nostrils shut, keeping your throat sealed with

Start equalizing the pressure in your ears while you are on the surface, before you dive under the water.

Continue clearing your ears every few feet as you descend.

your tongue, and gently "exhaling" (building pressure in your head) without actually letting any air escape. When you do this, you should hear your ears gently "pop."

You can't equalize effectively if you have a cold or allergies that cause your head to be "plugged" with mucous. If you have these problems, you must not dive below the surface or you risk rupturing your eardrum. Some days you may find that you just can't equalize, and if that is the case, you must not dive.

Start clearing your ears while you are on the surface, before you dive, and continue to clear them every few feet all the way to the bottom. Never wait until you feel pain or pressure on your eardrum to equalize the pressure in your ears. Pain is an indication that you have gone too far without equalizing. Repeated dives where you experience pain, but don't necessarily rupture your eardrum, will lead to some hearing loss over time.

Equalizing the pressure in your mask

As the pressure increases when you dive, it is also important to equalize the pressure in your mask. If you fail to equalize your mask, you will know the pressure is increasing because you will feel as if the mask is beginning to push into your face or form a suction. Continuing to descend with a mask that has not been equalized can cause the blood vessels in your eyes to rupture.

Most people equalize the pressure inside their masks without thinking about it, or do it accidentally when they equalize their ears. To ensure that you do not have a problem with your mask, blow a tiny bit of air into the mask as you descend until you just feel the mask move a fraction of an inch away from your face. You will need to repeat this action every few feet as you swim deeper underwater.

Diving underwater is easy

There are several different methods used to dive underwater quickly and easily. These techniques are known as the tuck dive, the pike dive, and the feet first or "kelp dive." Collectively, all three methods are used when you are in the water, on the surface, and are appropriately called "surface dives." They are all easy to do and you will be able to perform them with a small amount of practice.

The tuck dive is done when you are just lying on the surface, watching the bottom, looking for fish to photograph. You see a small, bright yellow fish dart out from a coral head and decide to dive down to it. To start the dive, you simply bend at the waist and throw your legs straight up into the air. The weight of your legs in the air will drive your body underwater.

The tuck dive is performed by bending at the waist and throwing your legs straight up into the air. The weight of your legs will help to drive you underwater.

Once your legs are completely underwater, start kicking and swim towards the bottom. Don't kick until your legs are underwater, however, as you will gain no propulsion from kicking in the air. In addition, if you kick while your fins are still on the surface, you will splash a great deal of water and noise will scare away the fish you want to photograph.

One of your goals as a skin diver is to make as little noise as possible. The more effectively you can dive without making noise, the more marine life you will see.

The pike dive or forward momentum dive is similar to the tuck dive, but is started as you swim on the surface.

Throw your legs up into the air as you bend at the waist and submerge your head and torso.

Once you have thrown your legs up into the air, do not start kicking until the tips of your fins are completely underwater.

The forward momentum dive, also known as the pike dive, is another effective way to dive beneath the surface. It's done the same way as the tuck dive except that rather than being motionless at the start of the dive, you swim to gain forward momentum, which will help propel you underwater even more efficiently. When you have reached the point where you want to dive, you throw your legs up into the air and the weight of your legs drives you toward the bottom.

The feet first dive, also known as the kelp dive, is used, as you might guess, when you are diving in thick kelp. Although kelp is usually thickly matted on the surface, you can swim between the individual stalks underwater.

To perform the dive, you start by resting vertically in the water. With your hands, you push the kelp away from your body, while turning in a circle, making an opening where you will descend.

Once you have created an opening, with your arms outstretched, you push down with your arms, bringing them in towards the side of your body, and keeping your arms in this position until submerged. At the same time you spread your legs and bring them together in a scissors kick. This combined action will drive your body up out of the water, where the weight of your body will make it sink below the surface.

To perform the kelp dive, spread the kelp, then spread your arms and legs and bring them together forcefully to drive your body up out of the water. The weight of your body will drive you under the water where you can turn and start swimming.

As your body becomes submerged, you can drive yourself deeper by raising your arms out to the side and lifting them over your head. When you are clear of the kelp mat you then rotate your body and turn head down to continue your dive.

Serious free divers will let the snorkel drop out of their mouth prior to descent. This allows the snorkel to fill completely with water at the very start of their dive, so that bubbles which might scare fish away do not vent from the snorkel while they are underwater.

Swimming underwater

For safety, it is strongly recommended that whenever you are swimming underwater that one member of your buddy team remains on the surface watching while the other person dives. In this way, you can easily alternate dives while one member of the team is catching his breath after a dive. If one person has a problem or passes out underwater, the other person is in a good position to help.

Whenever you are swimming underwater, it is a good idea for one member of the buddy team to remain on the surface.

While you are underwater, it is particularly important to regularly check your weight belt and make sure that it has not slipped around your waist and that the buckle is in the correct position. The deeper you dive, the more your wetsuit will compress, and the more likely it is that your belt will slide.

If for any reason you find yourself in an uncomfortable position underwater, where you have made a deep dive and are unsure whether you can reach the surface, take your belt off and hold it in your hand. By removing your belt, you virtually guarantee that you will rise to the surface if you pass out underwater, since your hand will relax and you'll drop the belt.

If you feel uncomfortable while you are underwater, take your weight belt off and hold it in your hand.

Surfacing from a dive

Any time you surface from a dive it is vital that you look up to ensure that there is nothing over you that you might hit with your head. If you fail to look up you could run into the bottom of the boat and knock yourself unconscious.

When the water is murky and underwater visibility is poor, it's necessary to keep your arm extended over your head to make sure you don't hit anything as you surface. It's better to hit the bottom of the boat with your hand than with your head!

Provided you are not diving in kelp, it's also essential to turn through a 360 degree circle as you surface to help avoid hitting any overhead objects. Don't do this in thick kelp, however, or you'll end up wrapping yourself up like a maypole!

Clearing the snorkel

Whenever you dive underwater, your snorkel will fill up completely with water. Fortunately, there is a very easy way

When you surface, you should look up, reach up with one arm and slowly turn in a circle to ensure there are no obstructions above you.

to clear the snork¢
you even get bac
surface. It's called ι
placement methoᴜ   oɾ
snorkel clearing.

When you are about six feet from breaking the surface, with your head tilted back, exhale a small puff of air into your snorkel. You should exhale just enough air for only a small amount of air to escape the snorkel. Until you get a feel for this, hold your hand gently at the back of the snorkel and feel the air coming out. The air

you have exhaled into the snorkel will "displace" the water.

When your head breaks the surface, snap it sharply forward and the snorkel will be clear of

To clear the snorkel by the displacement method, tilt your head back and exhale a puff of air into the snorkel when you are a few feet below the surface. Tilt your head sharply forward when you break the surface and the snorkel should clear of water.

water. It's that easy! Just be sure to promptly snap your head forward or the snorkel will fill with water again.

Of course, you can always clear your snorkel by exhaling sharply through it, but the displacement method is much easier and requires far less effort.

How to hold your breath for longer periods

Most people think that they won't be able to hold their breath for very long while they are underwater. Actually, you'll probably find that you can hold it for much longer than you might think, with just a bit of practice.

The first thing you must learn about extending your breath-hold time is to give your body time to adapt to the water. It takes your body about 20 minutes to adapt to being in the water and during this period your dives will be much shorter.

To effectively hold your breath you need to get your body into a rhythm. If you try to make each dive last until you feel an urgent need to breathe, you'll spend a long time on the surface recovering between each underwater excursion. It's far better to gradually extend each dive a little longer. Never push yourself to the point where you feel as though your lungs are "bursting" to breathe.

Ideally, your goal should be to try to spend an equal, or nearly equal, time underwater as you do on the surface. If you can spend a minute on the surface and a minute underwater you would be doing very well.

Another key to maximizing each dive is to learn to relax underwater and exert yourself as little as possible. If you are tense and worked up your body will be burning oxygen at a very fast rate. By relaxing and economizing your movements you will get the most time out of each dive.

Never hyperventilate!

Hyperventilation is a very dangerous technique that some divers use to extend their bottom time underwater. The consequences of hyperventilation are that it has killed many divers who have unexpectedly blacked out underwater.

Hyperventilation is defined as extremely rapid, forced, deep breathing. What this does to your body is it reduces your need to breathe to the point where you may actually pass out underwater due to a lack of oxygen, without ever feeling the need to breathe. This usually happens when a diver is returning to the surface, and since it occurs in shallow water it's known as "shallow water blackout."

Avoiding shallow water black-out is simple; don't hyperventilate. Breathe slowly without forcing your breathing in between surface dives. The extra few seconds you may gain by hyperventilating are not worth the risk it creates.

Establish positive buoyancy for surface swimming and resting

Whenever you are resting on the surface for more than a few minutes, or if you must swim on the surface for any distance, put just enough air in your snorkeling vest to make it easy for you to float. This will make it comfortable for you to rest and swim.

It shouldn't be necessary to inflate the vest completely to make yourself float easily. If you need to add more than a few puffs of air to the vest, then you're wearing too much weight. Inflating the vest completely will create "drag" and make it more difficult to swim on the surface. Add just enough air so that it is effortless for you to float.

To add air to the vest, you will need to either push down on the mouthpiece or pull up on it, depending on the design. Seal your lips around the stem and put a small amount of air into the vest at a time.

Blow enough air into the snorkeling vest so that you can rest easily on the surface.

CHAPTER 6

SNORKELING AND DIVING WITH CHILDREN

Most children who enjoy swimming love to go snorkeling and skin diving. Kids gets tremendously excited when they see a fish, a turtle, a crab, or just about any marine creature. To them, diving represents a tremendous adventure that they can participate in, and this is a great family activity that everyone can enjoy.

Of course, as in any water based activity, you must take certain common-sense precautions with children. They must be able to swim, and be comfortable swimming in a pool before you should ever consider taking them into open water. They also must understand that they must follow your directions explicitly at all times while in the water.

Selecting gear that fits

Although you might be tempted to get the least expensive equipment available for children because of the way they grow, think again. If you want children to enjoy the experience and you don't want to endanger them, they need good quality gear. It doesn't need to be as flashy as the equipment you might purchase for yourself, but it is essential that the gear fits them properly and is of a high enough quality that it will not break or otherwise fail to perform.

Snorkeling is a great family activity!

There are many good quality, smaller masks which are available for children today. Their mask must fit their face without leaking just as your mask should. Children will not usually outgrow a mask or snorkel for a few years.

Be sure the mask has a tempered lens, which is more resistant to breakage. In addition, if a tempered lens breaks it forms round "pebbles" of glass, rather than sharp shards.

Properly fitting gear is just as important for a child as it is for an adult.

Snorkels for children must be small enough to fit their mouths easily. It's especially important to make sure the snorkel is not too long. For a child, a snorkel should not be much longer than 12 inches.

It will generally be more economical to buy open heel adjustable fins for children than full foot fins. A child will outgrow a full foot fin very quickly, but an open heel adjustable fin will last for several seasons. Some open heel adjustable fins are available with padded inserts that can be removed as the child grows, allowing you to extend the useful life of the fin.

Getting children ready to snorkel

Before you take a child out into open water with mask, fins, and snorkel, it's a good idea for them to learn how to use the equipment in a pool first. While using fins is very natural, you will need to show your children how to properly don and adjust the fins so they don't lose them. You will probably need to assist them until they can do this themselves. Even then you'll probably still want to check their gear, at which time you can reinforce the buddy system by having them "check" your gear.

You'll also need to attach the snorkel to the mask and adjust the mask strap for your child. Smaller children may not appreciate the importance of making sure there is no hair inside the mask. You may need to help them with this.

Although it is not difficult to breathe through a snorkel, small children may have a difficult time clearing a snorkel or dealing with the sudden influx of water that occurs when a wave laps water into it. If the child can't clear the snorkel, make sure they understand that they can remove it from their mouth to drain the water out.

Once a child is at ease with the snorkeling gear in a pool you can make the transition with them to the ocean or lake. Don't try to make this move until the child indicates that they are ready to do so.

Maintaining close contact

It's vital to maintain close contact with children whenever you take them into an open water situation. The combination of glare on the water and

Children usually need help donning their equipment.

SNORKELING FUN

Be sure to maintain close contact with your child whenever they are in the water.

wind waves can make it impossible to see a small child even a short distance away. If there is any sort of a current it will be extremely difficult for a child to swim against it and they can easily be swept away.

One good way to help maintain contact with the child is to have them hold onto a surface float, like a boogie board, with a line attached to the float. Initially you may want to have the child lay on the float as you tow them around. However you use the float, you must have it available for the child to rest on if they become tired. There's always the chance that you may need to use the float yourself!

Most children are not able to skin dive down to any substantial depth, but they will dive repeatedly underwater. Before they begin to dive down to depths in excess of four or five feet they must understand how to equalize the pressure in their ears and the consequences that will occur if they fail to clear their ears.

Children have a natural curiosity which can override the caution normally demonstrated by adults. For this reason they must be closely supervised any time they are in the water.

Children get cold faster than adults

Although kids won't usually tell you they're cold, particularly if they're having a good time in the water, children usually chill much faster than adults. It's not uncommon for children to be shivering while they are in the water, yet still complain when ordered to get out. You must monitor your children, even in the tropics, to be sure they aren't getting too cold.

Wetsuits are available for children and although they grow out of them quickly, the added buoyancy they provide adds a degree of safety when a child is snorkeling. It's not usually a good idea to allow children to wear a weight belt until they demonstrate sufficient understanding and judgment for them to use one properly. Even then, children should be weighted so they are positively buoyant and float easily.

Watch out for dehydration

Make sure that children drink plenty of fluids, in both hot and cold weather. Children who are engrossed in snorkeling may not want to take the time to stop and have something to drink, so it's up to you to make sure they keep their fluid levels high.

Children are not always good about drinking enough fluids while snorkeling. Be sure they get plenty to drink.

Snorkeling and diving stimulate learning

Children will want to know what type of fish they are watching, what it eats, and where it goes when it swims away. You can use snorkeling and diving to stimulate their education and interest in a wide variety of subjects.

Try taking a child snorkeling on a shipwreck and you'll find it opens the doors to questions and learning about history. Give children simple underwater cameras to use and it can spark them to explore photography and biology. There is something in snorkeling and diving for almost everyone, and children will especially enjoy the experience.

CHAPTER 7

KEEPING SNORKELING FUN

Snorkeling and skin diving are adventures that take place in the outdoor environment, usually in the ocean or in a lake. Because these environments cannot be controlled, and because people make mistakes, accidents can and do occur. However, the number of snorkeling and skin diving accidents that happen each year is relatively small.

Almost all diving problems and accidents are avoidable when good judgment and safe diving practices are followed. In most instances, the key is prevention, by recognizing problems before they occur or as they develop.

Common watersport problems

Sunburn is undoubtedly the most common problem that affects snorkelers and skin divers. It's easy to forget that the sun is beating down on your back as you're absorbed in watching a beautiful reef scene below you. As the warm water laps over your body, you just don't realize how badly the sun is burning your skin.

Sunburn is easy to avoid, either through the use of waterproof sunblock or by wearing a dive skin or wetsuit. Even a T-shirt will provide protection for your back, although it won't protect the back of your legs or arms. Be sure to cover up so that you don't ruin your vacation through too much sun.

Caution should be used when applying waterproof sunblock to your face to avoid getting it too close to your eyes. Many of these lotions and creams will strongly irritate your eyes if you accidentally get it in them. Be sure to wait until the sunblock has dried completely before putting on your mask or going in the water.

Don't allow yourself to get exhausted

Although snorkeling and skin diving are relatively easy sports to enjoy, they do take physical effort. In addition, spending time in the water and the sun will subtly rob you of energy, especially if the water is cool. It's easy to become tired even though you're having fun.

To avoid exhaustion, if you're not in great shape, it's important to limit your time in the water and gradually lengthen your exposure in the water over several days. Start out with short exposures, depending on the water temperature.

In warm tropical waters, don't spend more than an hour at a time in the water without taking a rest on the beach or boat. In colder waters, a half hour to forty-five minutes can be a long time. Whatever you do, if you start getting chilled, get out of the water at the first opportunity.

If you find yourself getting exhausted in the water, and you're far from shore or the boat, there are several things that you can and should do. If you're really tired, and don't think you can make it back to the beach or the boat, drop your weight belt immediately. This will help you to establish positive buoyancy. In almost every case where a diver has drowned and they were wearing a weight belt at the start of the dive, the diver had failed to drop the belt when they became exhausted. The cost of the belt is insignificant compared to your safety.

If you are wearing a snorkeling vest, add just enough air to the vest to make yourself positively buoyant, but only after you have dropped your weight belt if you are wearing one. Relax, catch your breath, and slowly start swimming back to the shore or boat. For divers who are equipped with

With the snorkeling vest inflated, resting on the surface is effortless.

a boogie board or other float, get up on top of the float and rest until you have enough energy to swim back to safety.

Leg cramps can be painful but are easily relieved

When you are not accustomed to swimming with fins and you overdo it, it is easy to end up with cramps in your legs. Although they can be very painful, they are also easy to relieve.

To ease the pain of a cramp, straighten your leg as much as possible, then grab the tip of your fin and pull it towards you. This action will usually help relieve the cramp very quickly. Relax for a moment or try a different swimming position, such as on your back or side.

You can ease a cramp by yourself by straightening your leg as much as possible and pulling on your fin tip.

You can help your dive partner to relieve a cramp in a similar way. Have him relax on the surface on his back with his snorkel out of his mouth. Place your hand under his calf, grab the tip of his fin, and push the tip of the fin towards his body. Once the cramp is relieved he should rest for a few moments before trying to swim again and use a different swimming position from what he was using when the cramp set in.

Your snorkeling partner can help you ease a leg cramp quite easily.

Don't get dehydrated

Whenever you swim, snorkel, or dive, your body has a natural reaction to being immersed in the water, causing you to produce more urine than you would on land. The colder the water, the more pronounced this reaction and the more urine you will produce. When you urinate, you lose body water. If you're in the tropics and you sweat when you're out of the water, you lose additional moisture.

To avoid dehydration, it's important to drink more fluids than you would normally. Drink water, fruit juices, or soft drinks to restore lost fluids. Avoid alcohol prior to or during snorkeling.

Watch out for lines, nets, and aquatic plants

To avoid entanglement underwater, keep an eye out for lines, nets, and aquatic plants. These objects can become snagged on your gear, but it's usually a simple matter to disengage them and clear yourself.

Although it's rare for divers to become completely tangled up in kelp or lines, these obstructions become more of a problem when the water is murky and visibility is poor. This is one reason why divers carry knives with them underwater.

There are specific techniques for skin diving in and around kelp which are easy to learn and will help you avoid entanglement. In California, the most interesting diving is in the kelp, because this is where most of the marine life is found.

To avoid having your gear snag on anything underwater, it's important to streamline your equipment as much as possible. Any piece of gear that sticks out at an odd angle can snag on seaweed, coral, parts of a shipwreck, and similar items. Streamlining will also help you to swim more quickly and easily.

If you do find yourself caught on some type of obstruction, it's important to remain calm and not panic. Usually, if you back up slowly, the snag will free itself, but if you panic and thrash about, you may make your situation worse.

When backing up doesn't free you, carefully use your knife to cut the obstruction away. You can also try dropping your weight belt if you are wearing one. In a situation like this, a competent diving partner who is watching you from the surface is invaluable.

Drowning is a risk of snorkeling and skin diving

Drowning is a risk for anyone who plays in or on the water, but most drownings occur because people violate one or more water safety rules. In snorkeling and skin diving, you wear equipment that helps make swimming easier. However, this equipment should not be a crutch for poor swimming ability. You must be able to survive in the water comfortably even if you lose your mask, fins, and snorkel.

As long as you are floating on the surface your chances of drowning are greatly reduced. For this reason, when you are not swimming underwater, you should always maintain positive buoyancy through careful weighting or the use of your snorkeling vest. If you find yourself exhausted, your first action should always be to get rid of any weights that you are wearing. In most cases, they can be recovered later.

As mentioned previously, if you should ever feel faint or otherwise unwell while you are in the water, take your weight belt off and hold it in your hand. If you pass out, you'll drop the belt and be floating on the surface.

Every snorkeler and skin diver should take a water safety course as well as a CPR (cardio pulmonary resuscitation) and first aid course. If you have children who snorkel or skin dive, these courses become doubly important.

When you are swimming on the surface, maintain positive buoyancy so that floating is easy.

Skin Diving Problems

Eardrum rupture and shallow water blackout can only occur if you are a skin diver who dives beneath the surface. Snorkelers who never submerge more than their face in the water do not have to deal with either of these potential problems. Both problems are easily avoided as discussed in the chapter on skin diving skills.

CHAPTER 8

WHERE TO GO SNORKELING

You can enjoy snorkeling and breath-hold diving almost any place there is clear water. The most crucial elements to your enjoyment will be water with good visibility and interesting things to see underwater.

The better the underwater visibility, the more you will enjoy snorkeling.

When snorkelers and divers talk about visibility they normally describe it in terms of how many feet they can see underwater. Since conditions vary from location to location, how good the visibility appears is a relative term. For example, in California, the visibility is generally considered to be good if you are able to see anything over 30 feet away underwater. However, in the tropics, if you could only see a distance of 30 feet the conditions might be considered "poor." Average underwater visibility in the tropics is usually 50-75 feet with exceptional days in excess of 100 feet. In certain extraordinary locations you may be able to see up to 200 feet underwater!

When you hear snorkelers and divers talk about the "viz," they're referring to the visibility. If you want to be "hip," this is the term to use!

The visibility at any underwater site can change radically, sometimes in just a few hours. Weather is normally the biggest factor affecting visibility, including surface waves, breaking surf (at ocean sites), and sun, but it can also be affected by marine life.

Extend courtesy to swimmers and boaters

In your enthusiasm for snorkeling it's sometimes easy to forget that there are other people with whom you must share popular watersport sites. For example, many areas that are popular for snorkeling are also popular for swimming. As a snorkeler, it's important to be courteous to other people around you in the water, especially to avoid running into them accidentally as you dive or surface from a dive.

Any time there is boat traffic, it is especially important to make sure that you do not put yourself in the path of oncoming vessels. Never snorkel or dive in a ship channel or near a dock.

Always be sure to fly the diver's down flag when you are snorkeling or skin diving, but remember not to expect that every boat operator knows or recognizes this flag. Keep a sharp eye out for boat traffic and be prepared to move out of the way quickly. A snorkeler with only his head sticking out of the water can be very difficult to see.

Personal watercraft (sometimes known as jet skis) also pose a serious hazard to snorkelers because many times the people who operate these craft have only rented them and do not know the rules for safe boat operation. Be especially careful if people are operating personal watercraft in the area.

Lakes, rivers, and streams can provide adventures close to home

Just because you don't live close to the ocean doesn't mean that there aren't places to go snorkeling and skin diving close by. Any clear lake, river, or stream can provide interesting opportunities to explore underwater.

Snorkeling in lakes can be interesting and enjoyable.

Fresh water snorkeling sites typically don't have the variety of creatures that you will find in the ocean, but there are still fish, turtles, crayfish, aquatic plants, and many other interesting things to watch. The best way to know what there is to see and where to snorkel in your local area is to visit one of the local dive stores. These stores will also frequently have maps or books that cover the local sites.

Shipwrecks in fresh water are usually in much better condition than those found in salt water. At sites like Isle Royale National Park in the Great Lakes, some of the wrecks lie in water as shallow as four feet, sloping off to deeper depths. Almost everything on these wrecks is perfectly pre served.

Snorkeling for crayfish is a fun way to spend an afternoon as a prelude to a great dinner. You can make a day of an event like this.

The visibility at fresh water snorkeling sites is usually not quite as good as it is at salt water sites, although there are exceptions. Check with your local dive store to find out when conditions are likely to be good.

Ocean waters offer the greatest variety of aquatic life

You will see the greatest variety of aquatic life when you snorkel in the ocean. The colors, shapes, and habits of marine life must be seen up close to be fully appreciated.

Marine life identification books and waterproof marine life i.d. cards are available for both warm and cold water snorkeling locations. These books are geared toward the snorkeler and diver, telling you where to look for these creatures and a bit about their habits and lives.

Tropical diving offers warm, clear water

Many people get their first exposure to snorkeling during a vacation to a tropical site like Hawaii or the Caribbean. These locations offer a dazzling array of fish, corals, and other creatures.

The typical tropical snorkeling site will consist of a coral reef, surrounded by sand channels, and swarming with brightly colored fish. The reef may be one large area or there may be scattered clumps of coral.

Coral reefs are formed by tiny creatures called

Coral reefs swarm with hundreds of brightly colored fish.

"polyps" which secrete a hard external skeleton, building the reef layer by layer. Brittle and delicate, corals must not be touched or they will be damaged and die.

As you swim above the reef you will see sea fans and sea whips swaying in the currents. These are not plants as you might suppose, rather they are animals related to the corals. Again, these creatures are delicate and should not be handled.

Sponges grow in both cold and warm waters, although the sponges that live in the tropics generally are larger and more colorful than those found in colder seas. Like corals, sponges are living creatures that live by filtering water

Sponges come in many different shapes and sizes.

through their bodies and extracting microscopic bits of food.

There are many different types of fish found living on coral reefs, ranging from tiny, brightly colored butterfly fish to massive groupers weighing several hundred pounds. Watching the antics of the fish is what makes snorkeling fascinating.

"Cleaner fish" actually clean small parasites off much larger fish, who line up along the reef for this service. Silversides are small, highly reflective fish that form huge schools that live inside caves or wrecks. Fairy basslets are brightly colored yellow and purple fish that often swim upside down along the underside of ledges or crevices. Learning to identify these fish and to understand their habits makes snorkeling more interesting.

WHERE TO GO SNORKELING   **93**

Groupers are large fish that may grow up to several hundred pounds.

Fish such as parrotfish feed on coral, chewing up the hard external skeleton to get at the delicate polyps inside. Spotted drums have long, ribbon-like fins that undulate as they swim. Triggerfish are small aggressive fish that protect their territory and nests and will actually try to chase you away from their turf.

Larger open ocean creatures (frequently referred to as "pelagics") will occasionally visit the edges of the reef, providing a real thrill as they swim in to check you out. These creatures include manta rays, whale sharks, and the larger tunas.

Cold water snorkeling sites are worth visiting, too

The cool waters of southern California or New England are worth visiting if you enjoy snorkeling. Although these sites may require you to use a wetsuit to be comfortable, they have much to offer. The corals which make up the underwater habitat are not found in colder waters, but a different set of creatures make snorkeling and skin diving just as interesting.

Swimming through a kelp bed is like swimming through a giant redwood forest. As the sun filters down through the kelp you will catch glimpses of the calico bass, orange garibaldi, and sheephead swimming along the rocky reef.

California kelp beds are home to many different creatures. The kelp grows rapidly in the nutrient rich waters found on the west coast. Here you can see the individual bulbs of the kelp plant.

The bright orange garibaldi is commonly seen in the kelp forest.

The sheep-head is a large toothy fish that can be found at many snorkeling spots.

Kelp anchors itself to the bottom in most locations by attaching itself to the rocks, and this is the area where you will see the most marine life. Some animals such as halibut, stingrays, and sand dollars live out on the sand, but the more colorful creatures tend to live on the rocks and in the kelp.

Lobsters and crabs also live among the rocks and tend to hide in holes during the daytime hours, coming out at night to feed. Many different species of anemones, which resemble brightly colored flowers, but are really animals, also live on the reef.

Some of the most interesting creatures to be found in colder waters are the seals, sea lions, and whales which frequent these environments. These animals will frequently swim right up to you, spinning and diving at high speed.

Planning your snorkeling adventure

Wherever you go snorkeling, it's always important to take a few moments to plan what you will do before you enter the water. Talk about your activity with your snorkeling partner. Discuss where you will go and how long you intend to stay in the water. Look for other points where you can exit the water if you are unable to return to the point where you first entered.

If you are diving in the ocean, whether you are diving from the beach or a boat, you must plan your dive according to the sea conditions. The most important factor in planning for snorkeling will be whether or not there is a current.

Currents are like rivers of water within the ocean and they can have tremendous strength. If the current is strong, you will not be able to swim against it, no matter what your swimming ability may be. If the current is mild, you can still go snorkeling, but you must always take it into consideration in your planning.

If there is a mild current, plan to snorkel up current at the start of your snorkeling excursion, so that you can return to your exit point with the current and not struggle against it. This will help you avoid exhaustion.

If, for any reason, you feel uncomfortable about the diving conditions on a particular day, don't get in the water. It is not uncommon for even highly experienced professional divers to call off a dive because they feel sometimes the conditions are not right for diving.

Entering the water from the beach

Entering the water from the beach is a popular way to get into the water for snorkeling. If you plan to snorkel in a lake where there are no waves, you simply don most of your gear on shore, except for your fins, and wade out into the water to let the water support you while you don your flippers.

For beach diving in the ocean, it's usually easiest to don all of your gear except your fins at your car rather than dragging your gear down to the beach to get dressed. This has the added advantage that you will usually get a lot less sand inside your equipment by dressing in at the car.

For beach diving, it is usually easiest to don your gear at your car, rather than dragging your equipment down to the beach.

If you are going to snorkel in the ocean, you can don your fins in the water, provided there is no surf. If there are any waves at all, it is much safer to don your fins on the beach. You must also perform a proper "surf entry" if there are any waves to avoid injury and losing equipment.

Look for rocks and other hazards in the surf zone. These obstacles should be avoided. If there are surfers or lots of swimmers, look for another place to enter the water. A collision with a surfboard can ruin your day!

Don your fins at the water's edge by standing up and leaning on your buddy as you don one fin at a time. When you are both ready and have decided it's time to enter the water, put your mask on your face and your snorkel in your mouth. Enter the water by shuffling your feet and walking sideways out through the surf.

If there is any surf, it is essential to don all your gear on the beach before entering the water.

To prepare for a surf entry, you must first watch the waves so that you can time your entry and avoid going into the water when the surf is large. Waves normally arrive at the beach in sets, with several small waves followed by several larger waves. Watch the surf and count the sets until you see a pattern. You want to enter the water at the start of a small set of waves.

If you try to walk forward in the water while wearing fins you'll quickly find you can't do it and you may stumble and hurt yourself. Although it is easy to walk backwards with fins on, it's never a good idea to turn your back on the ocean, since the giant wave of the day may suddenly appear and crash down on you.

Hold onto your mask as you enter the water to avoid losing it if you fall or a wave breaks over you. If a large wave appears as you are entering the water, dive underneath it while holding your mask.

Be sure not to get in front of or behind your buddy when entering or exiting the water. If a large wave should break it could throw you against each other and injure both of you.

Hold your mask as you shuffle your feet sideways and move out through the surf.

Never stop in the surf zone, the area where the waves are breaking. If you do, it's very likely that you will lose some or all of your equipment. If you lose a piece of equipment because of the surf, it's unlikely that you will find it again. Either move back to the beach or out past the waves, but don't stop in the surf and try to find your lost gear. You'll just end up losing even more gear!

As soon as the water is deep enough to swim, turn so that you are facing toward the open sea, drop into the water,

Start swimming as soon as the water is deep enough. Do not stop in the surf zone.

and start kicking hard away from the beach. Don't stop kicking until you are outside of the surf zone. Once you are past the waves, you can stop and rest.

Returning to the beach

If there is no surf, it's a simple matter to return to the beach. Simply swim in until the water is waist deep, stand up, remove your fins, and walk out.

You must plan your exit carefully if there is any surf. Without proper planning you will lose equipment and may injure yourself. Surf exits are easier than entries but they must be done properly.

Prior to exiting the water, stop just outside the surf line and monitor the waves again until you see a pattern of large and small sets of waves begin to emerge. Start your swim into the beach at the start of the small set.

Swim as fast as you can towards the beach, keeping an eye out for waves breaking behind you. If a wave starts to break under you, ride the wave into the beach by bodysurfing it. Lock your hands together out ahead of you and hold your body rigid like a surfboard as you ride on the crest of the wave.

If a wave breaks behind you or is about to break on top of you, hold your mask tightly on your face and dive underneath the wave back out towards the sea. As soon as you surface, resume your swim towards shore.

Back out of the water, keeping an eye on the surf.

Once you are in water shallow enough stand up, put your feet on the bottom and start backing out, facing the waves, with your back to the beach. Back out as quickly as you can. Do not remove any of your equipment while you are in the water.

If for some reason you fall down as you are backing out, stay down and do not attempt to stand up again. Crawl out of the surf on your hands and knees until you are up on the beach and can remove your gear, before you stand up again.

Watch the primary current flow

At most snorkeling sites, there is a primary direction in which the current normally flows. For example, along the California coast, the primary current flow is from north to south. A snorkeler who enters the northern end of a beach and doesn't watch the current, will usually gradually drift towards the southern end of the beach.

Always keep your eye on the current by watching which way the kelp is drifting or looking at other objects floating on the surface. Keep in mind that currents can become completely slack or reverse directions entirely over a short period of time.

Avoiding rip currents

Rip currents are currents of water running off the beach in a channel out to sea. The water in the rip moves extremely fast, much faster than you can swim.

Rip currents may occur due to temporary conditions, although they may last for several hours. Temporary rips usually form when the water creates a channel in the sand which allows the sea to rush back out through this conduit.

Permanent rip currents are found near some piers or where the water runs out from shore between a sandbar or gap in a reef. The force of the water running through the cut in the bar or reef is tremendous.

Most rips run in a 90 degree angle away from the shore. If you are caught in a rip, don't try to swim against it.

Either ride it out until it stops or swim out of the rip at a 90 degree angle, parallel to the beach. If there is a current running along the beach, swim out of the rip by swimming down current.

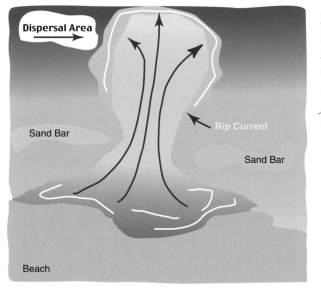

Diagram of a typical rip current as it would be seen from above.

What is undertow?

Undertow occurs when there is big surf and water runs off a steep beach back out towards sea. If the undertow is strong enough, it can pull your feet out from underneath you as you try to enter the water or exit the ocean to the beach.

Certain beaches are notorious for their undertow and should be avoided unless you have extensive beach diving experience. The ocean is much more powerful than you and must be respected.

Be aware of changing conditions

Whenever you are in the water, you must be aware of changing conditions around you. No matter where you snorkel, conditions can change very rapidly and you must be vigilant to know when it is time to get out of the water.

Beach diving means sand in your gear

Probably the most negative part of beach diving is dealing with the sand that gets in your equipment. This is usually unavoidable. Just be sure to take the time to thoroughly rinse your gear as soon as possible after diving.

Boat diving is easy

Boat diving is ordinarily much easier than beach diving. You do not need to contend with sand, rocks, surf, or long hikes down to the beach. Most snorkelers prefer boat diving rather than beach diving, unless they are prone to seasickness.

Almost any type of boat will work for snorkeling, from large boats to small inflatables. In most cases, the larger the boat, the more comfortable it will be as a dive platform. Larger charter boats that take snorkeling groups out to explore tropical reefs are frequently equipped with bathrooms, showers, and food service. Smaller boats are not normally as well equipped.

Snorkeling from a large boat

Snorkeling from a large boat is usually quite easy. There will be space to store your dry belongings, like your clothes, and sufficient room to get dressed into your gear.

If you're staying at a hotel that does not have its own dive operation, the boat operator will usually operate a bus to pick up snorkelers at each hotel. Be sure to be on time or the bus will leave without you. They won't come looking for you, and you'll be out the price of your trip since they have reserved space for you that could have been sold to another customer.

If you drive your own car to the charter boat, it is still essential to be on board a few minutes before the boat is scheduled to depart. If you don't know exactly where the boat

If you're staying at a hotel that provides bus service to a boat, be sure to be on time for the bus. The driver won't come looking for you if you're late, and you'll be out the price of a trip.

is going to leave from, allow yourself enough extra time to find the boat. Charter boats depart promptly and will not wait for tardy customers. It's your responsibility to be on the boat with all of your equipment when it pulls away from the dock.

During the ride out to the snorkeling site, get your gear ready to go so that you will be able to enter the water promptly and not waste time fumbling with your equipment.

Be sure to have all your gear with you when you board the boat. If you are late for the boat for any reason the captain will not wait for you.

Be sure to drink some fluids, especially if the weather is warm.

At the dive site, the divemaster will give a briefing on the site and point out where you should go and the things you should see, as well as any areas to avoid. Pay attention to the divemaster's directions because he will know the site intimately and is watching out for your safety and enjoyment.

Listen to the divemaster. He will point out the best areas on the reef, as well as those areas you may want to avoid.

Some boats will take scuba divers and snorkelers out on the same trip. If you are on a trip with scuba divers, be sure to stay out of their way, especially when they are entering or exiting the water. They cannot move as fast as you can and their equipment is heavy. Having a scuba diver fall on you will be painful at best.

Snorkelers customarily enter the water from an area known as the "dive door" or the "gate", which is an opening on the side of the boat that is low to the water and unobstructed. Other boat operators may have a large "swim step" which is used for both entering and exiting the water.

To enter the water from a large boat, the most frequent way to enter is known as the "giant stride entry." Prepare for the entry by donning all of your equipment, but don't put

To enter the water from a large boat, the most common entry used is known as the "giant stride" entry.

your fins on until you are right at the entry point. Once you have donned your fins, stand up at the edge of the boat with your fins over the edge as far as possible. Make sure there is no one in the water below you. Hold your mask with one hand and if you're wearing a weight belt hold the buckle with your other hand. Take a giant step off the edge of the boat, but don't hop or leap. Just step off.

Once you sink in the water up to your waist, bring your legs together to help prevent your body from sinking any deeper in the water. Check your mask strap to be sure that it has not slipped to the top of your head. Move away from the entry point so that your snorkeling partner can enter the water without landing on top of you, and watch your partner enter the water.

Snorkeling from a small boat

If you're snorkeling from a small boat which is privately owned and not normally used for snorkeling, the first thing to check is to be sure there is a ladder or some other method of getting back aboard the boat. If there isn't a way to get back aboard easily, you should think twice about getting into the water!

Another important consideration if you are snorkeling from a small private boat is to be sure there is a "current line" available to help you get back to the boat. A current line is a length of floating line, usually about 100 feet long and made from polypropylene, with a float or buoy attached to one end. The line is secured to the boat and streams out with the current. In the event you are swept past the boat by a strong current, the current line can be used to help pull yourself back to the boat.

There are several ways to enter the water from a small boat, but the two most common methods are the

If you are snorkeling from a private boat, be sure to use a current line so you have a way to help pull yourself back to the boat if there is a current.

Use the current line to pull yourself back to the boat.

"backwards roll," or by simply lowering yourself into the water if the distance from the water to the boat is low. Whichever method is comfortable for you is acceptable.

To do a backwards roll, don all your gear and sit on the side of the boat with your feet inside the boat and your back facing the water. Make sure that there is no one in the water below you. Hold your mask against your face with one hand and simply roll backwards off the boat.

Be sure to wait until you stop rolling before you start swimming, because it is easy to swim into the side of the boat and hit your head if you're not careful. Check your mask strap before releasing your hold on your mask to ensure that the strap has not come off the back of your head, otherwise you may lose your mask.

The back- wards roll is one of the most com- mon entries used to get in the water when snor- keling from a small boat.

Lowering yourself into the water works best on boats that are very low to the water, such as an inflatable or small fiberglass boat. With all your gear on, sit on the side of the boat with your feet in the water. Use your arms to gradually lower yourself into the water, as your back slides against the side of the boat.

Getting back aboard the boat

If the boat is equipped with a ladder, getting back aboard is a simple matter. First, wait until the ladder is completely clear, so that you aren't underneath anyone who may be boarding the boat. If the boat pitches and they lose their grip they could fall on top of you and seriously injure you.

While holding onto the ladder, remove one fin at a time and hand them up into the boat. Be sure to hold onto the ladder tightly, because once you remove your fins it will be more difficult to swim, especially if there is a current.

Once you have removed your fins, climb the ladder and clear the area so that the next snorkeler can get back on board. Don't stand around in the boarding area, but clear the area immediately.

Take your fins off and hand them back aboard the boat before you climb the ladder. Be sure to hold onto the ladder with one hand as you remove your fins.

If the boat does not have a ladder, you can also boost yourself back on board, just the way you would at the side of a swimming pool in deep water. Hold onto the sides of the boat, kick vigorously with your legs, and lift yourself up with your arms. Swing either leg up over the side and rotate your body to a sitting position on the side of the boat.

If the boat is not equipped with a ladder you can boost yourself back in over the side, provided the boat is low enough to the water. This technique can be difficult or impossible to use if you are snorkeling out of a sailboat.

CHAPTER 9

MAKING FRIENDS WITH MARINE LIFE

One of the most exciting aspects of snorkeling is the opportunity to get close to and observe different types of marine animals. Almost everywhere that you can snorkel there will be interesting animals to observe.

Most marine creatures are quite shy and tend to be afraid of people, particularly if you splash and make lots of noise in the water. However, some animals will allow you to approach them very closely while other creatures will actually take the initiative and approach you.

No matter how friendly a marine creature may appear, you must always remember that these are wild animals and as such, their behavior is unpredictable. Although you might think of a dolphin or a whale as a "friendly" creature, and they usually are harmless, these are large, powerful animals that are capable of hurting you, either accidentally or intentionally if they become annoyed or frightened. Even "cute" and "cuddly" creatures such as sea otters and sea lions have been known to bite divers, and these creatures have sharp, canine teeth which can inflict painful wounds.

During mating season, marine mammals such as whales, dolphins, and sea lions can become extremely territorial and aggressive. Female marine mammals are also quite protective of their young.

Marine mammals in the U.S. are protected by the Federal Marine Mammal Protection Act which outlines specific guidelines on human interaction with marine mammals in U.S. waters. It is illegal to harass marine mammals in any way.

Feeding fish is fun

Feeding fish can be fun, but it can also lead to cuts and injuries. Even small species of fish can have sharp teeth that can cut your skin and cause you to bleed. At least one diver has been bitten by a barracuda who had become accustomed to being hand fed and mistook a hand signal by the fingers of the diver for a piece of fish. Keep in mind that any time you feed fish you can be accidentally injured.

Some of the marine creatures that you will encounter may surprise you with their friendliness, but most will be shy. Be sure to respect the space of any animal who retreats from you and never corner a marine creature under circumstances where they have no escape.

In this chapter we'll take a look at some of the more interesting marine creatures you may have the chance to encounter, as well as some that require you to be somewhat cautious.

The smile of the dolphin

Man has interacted with dolphins for hundreds of years and swimming with these beautiful creatures in the open ocean is a magical experience. Their grace and beauty must be seen to be believed.

There are captive dolphin programs where you can swim with dolphins that are held in pens, but to truly appreciate these animals you must swim with them in the wild. Several dive charter operators in Florida run special trips to the Caribbean where you have the opportunity to snorkel with

Dolphins may become attached to a particular person and ignore all other humans in the area as they focus on this individual.
(© Doug Perrine/Innerspace Visions)

wild dolphins. The behavior of dolphins in a marine aquarium will not necessarily be like the behavior of dolphins in the wild.

Like all marine mammals, dolphins breathe air and must surface regularly to do so. They usually live in pods which may include males, females, and baby dolphins.

In many instances, dolphins will become attached to a particular person, who they may approach more closely, ignoring other snorkelers. This will be their choice, not yours. Dolphins have also been known to be physically aggressive with humans.

Manatees are shy

Manatees are another type of air breathing aquatic mammal which are found in the fresh water springs of Florida. These slow moving creatures feed on aquatic plants and are quite shy and docile. They are a protected species and must not be harassed.

Manatees are extremely vulnerable to fast moving boats, and every year a good number of them are injured by careless boat operators. In most areas, access to the manatees is restricted and they cannot be approached. The law requires that you not chase the manatees, but allow the creatures to come to you.

Check state laws in Florida for the latest regulations regarding access to the manatees. Severe fines can be imposed for violating the regulations.

The waters where the manatees live are cool and you will want to wear a wetsuit if you intend to spend more than a few minutes in the water. Swimming with the manatees is an exceptional experience for any snorkeler.

Manatees are shy, docile creatures.   *(© Doug Perrine/Innerspace Visions)*

The grace of rays

There are many different species of rays, ranging from the largest manta rays down to very small stingrays. These are shy, gentle creatures that will often avoid contact with snorkelers.

Rays are related to sharks and skates in that they are all "cartilaginous" fish, i.e., they do not have bones, they have cartilage. Different types of rays are found in virtually every area of the world.

Manta rays live in the open ocean, although they will occasionally come into relatively shallow water to feed.

They are filter feeders, eating microscopic animals and plants known as "plankton."

Mantas are incredibly graceful animals and powerful swimmers. They can be curious and will sometimes deliberately interact with divers and snorkelers. They have no stinger and are generally considered to be harmless.

Manta rays are graceful creatures that can swim quite rapidly when they are alarmed.   *(© Doug Perrine/Innerspace Visions)*

Mantas can grow up to 22 feet in width and weigh up to several tons! It is not uncommon to see a type of suckerfish, known as a remora, attached to a manta, hitching a free ride.

Stingrays are much smaller creatures than mantas, but they are equally graceful and appear in varied colors and shapes. Stingrays are named for their stinger or "barb" which is located on their tail. This is a defensive "weapon" only, which the stingray will use if attacked by a shark. These animals normally live on sandy bottoms in relatively shallow water.

If you were to accidentally step on a stingray, there is a good chance that you would be injured by the reflex action of the stinger which is attached to the tail. This is purely a defensive measure on the ray's part. To avoid this type of

At Stingray City on Grand Cayman you can hand feed stingrays in shallow water.

accident, shuffle your feet if you are entering the water from a sandy beach.

At Grand Cayman Island in the Caribbean there is a dive site known as Stingray City, where snorkelers can hand feed stingrays. The island fishermen cleaned their fish at this site for many years and the stingrays would congregate there to feed on the remains. Divers found out about this site and began to organize daily trips to feed the stingrays. This is one of the most exciting snorkeling adventures you can enjoy in less than five feet of water.

Each snorkeler is given a container of chopped up squid to feed the rays. The rays hear the boat's anchor and are usually waiting under the boat as you enter the water. They glide over your body, searching for the squid, which they locate by smell.

The belly of a stingray is as soft as velvet. You can touch these creatures and gently stroke them. This is a fantastic dive for underwater photography because the water is shallow and the stingrays and fish are all over.

Feeding a stingray is like feeding a horse. You hold the squid out with your hand flat. If you're not careful, your fingers can get sucked into the ray's mouth. Although they do not have teeth, they do have grinding "plates," which are used to crush clams and other small shellfish. If your fingers get sucked into their mouth you can lose skin and it can be a bit painful, but most people don't let a bit of discomfort interfere with the experience!

Thousands of divers and snorkelers have experienced Stingray City and many people have returned to enjoy the adventure over and over again. If you have the opportunity to visit this site, don't miss it!

Sharks are sleek and beautiful creatures

Under normal circumstances, most snorkelers will rarely ever have the opportunity to see a shark, let alone encounter one that is dangerous. There are numerous different types of sharks, but few are known to cause problems for snorkelers. Unless you visit certain specific locations, your chance of seeing a shark is remote.

Most of the more common sharks will avoid snorkelers, especially in the shallow waters where most snorkeling is done. It is quite possible to enjoy snorkeling for many years and never glimpse a shark.

The most common shark that you may see while diving in the tropics is the nurse shark, which is a docile animal that spends most of its time sleeping on the bottom or in holes in the reef. Nurse sharks do have sharp teeth, however, and should not be harassed because they have been known to bite divers who have pulled their tails or otherwise annoyed them.

The angel shark resembles a stingray more than it does a shark.

In cold water, such as off California, you may see the horn shark, the leopard shark, the swell shark, or the angel shark, which is a flattened shark which lives on the bottom. None of these sharks are aggressive, although like the nurse shark, the angel shark will bite if you antagonize it.

Most sharks are not aggressive towards people in any way.

In many places in the world today, scuba divers and snorkelers pay money to dive with sharks in situations where the sharks have been "baited," deliberately attracted by food so that the sharks can be seen and photographed. Hundreds of dives are done like this each year, confirming that the sharks are primarily interested only in their natural food, which is fish. They are not normally interested in people.

Of course, there are several species of sharks that are highly aggressive and dangerous to man, such as great white sharks and tiger sharks. However, the odds of encountering this type of shark are quite low. Great white sharks feed primarily on marine mammals, such as elephant seals, sea lions, and harbor seals. White sharks are most commonly found near "rookeries," where hundreds of marine mammals gather to breed. Skin diving near these areas is extremely hazardous and should be avoided.

Certain areas are known to be frequented by great white sharks and these locations have been the sites of attacks on skin and scuba divers. Areas in California that are frequented by white sharks include the Farallon Islands, the mouth of Tomales Bay, and the western tip of San Miguel Island. These are all sites with large populations of marine mammals.

Tiger sharks are found in tropical waters, but are rarely seen even in these locations. They spend most of their time in the open ocean, but will come into shallow water to feed on occasion.

If you see a shark and it makes you nervous, exit the water slowly and deliberately, while keeping an eye on the shark. In most cases, unless you have been spearfishing and are towing wounded or bleeding fish (which is not recommended), the shark will not be interested in you and will quickly disappear.

The largest species of shark is the whale shark. These docile animals are filter feeders and eat plankton, the smallest living creatures in the sea.

Whale sharks feed on tiny microscopic animals.
(© Ben Cropp/ Innerspace Visions)

Barracudas are inquisitive

Barracudas are highly curious creatures that will follow snorkelers for hours. They have long cylindrical bodies and are quite silvery in color. Their toothy grin gives them a fearsome appearance, but it is extremely rare for them to nip at a diver unless he is carrying speared fish.

The great barracuda, as this fish is more properly named, is found throughout the world in tropical seas. If approached, they will back away and retreat.

Barracudas grow to a maximum size of about six feet. These are dramatic creatures which should be respected, but you should not be concerned if you see one while snorkeling.

Barracudas are inquisitive fish which will retreat when followed.

Torpedo rays can be shocking

Most snorkelers will probably never see a torpedo ray. One species of torpedo ray is found off Florida and the Yucatan peninsula in Mexico, while a second type is found off the west coast of the U.S. and as far south as central Baja.

Torpedo rays are known for their ability to produce a strong electric current which they use to stun small fish which they eat. These rays will also use their shocking power as a defensive mechanism and can be quite aggressive. Where most normal rays (other than those at Stingray City) will get out of your way underwater, torpedo rays swim around as if they own the ocean. While they generally won't attack a snorkeler, if you are in their way and don't move, you might get a shock from them. The larger the ray, the more serious the jolt.

Torpedo rays can deliver a stiff electrical charge.

Torpedo rays are fairly uncommon, but you can recognize them by their round body and tail (they have no stinger), and their "in-your-face" attitude. They are usually gray or brown with spots. If a torpedo ray swims towards you, you normally will have plenty of time to get out of its way, as they are ordinarily slow swimmers.

Seals and sea lions love to play

Seals and sea lions are small marine mammals which are common on the west coast of the U.S. They are curious creatures and will often follow snorkelers for extended periods of time. Although they are somewhat similar in appearance, seals and sea lions are distinctly different animals.

Seals are smaller than sea lions and tend to be more timid and gentle. They have no external ears and small front flippers, which makes it difficult for them to walk on land. Their coat is spotted and their eyes are large relative to their head.

Harbor seals are found all along the Pacific coast, but especially at the offshore islands, such as Catalina, Anacapa, Santa Cruz, Santa Barbara, and San Miguel. They are curious animals and will sometimes approach quite closely.

Sea lions are larger, more aggressive creatures that have visible external ears. Both their front and rear flippers are quite large, allowing them to move easily along a beach or climb onto rocks.

Sea lions are much faster and more agile swimmers than seals. It is not uncommon for them to swim at high speed at a snorkeler and then veer off at the last possible moment. During mating season, the males will swim very close and bare their sharp teeth. When sea lions display aggressive behavior like this, it's best to get out of their way.

Seal and sea lion pups can be highly curious and may approach you quite closely. It's best to avoid touching them. To avoid a possible negative situation, never get between a pup and its mother.

Harbor seals will sometimes tug on a snorkeler's fin under-water.

Sea lions are fast swimmers. They can be quite aggressive during mating season.

MAKING FRIENDS WITH MARINE LIFE

Lionfish have a delicate beauty

Lionfish are among the most beautiful and interesting fish found in the Indo-Pacific region. They live in caves and crevices and have broad, "leafy" fins.

The spines of the lionfish are highly poisonous. Although these fish will not attack a snorkeler or diver, like the torpedo ray, they seem to understand that they are well protected. They swim slowly and confidently, and generally will not back down if another fish approaches them. They are definitely a fish with an "attitude."

Watch them, enjoy them, and photograph them as much as you please, but do not try to handle or touch a lionfish. The puncture wounds from their spines are extremely painful.

Lionfish have poisonous spines they use strictly for defense. They are not aggressive creatures.

Moray eels breathe through their mouths

Moray eels look fearsome! This is because they breathe through their open mouths, exposing their needle-like teeth. Despite their ferocious appearance, they are actually shy creatures that rarely come out of their holes during daytime hours.

Different species of morays are found in almost every sea and their colors are highly varied. There are green morays, spotted morays, banded morays, and numerous other color variations.

Morays will usually retreat if you approach them closely, but if they are harassed they will not hesitate to bite. Skin divers sometimes get bitten when they put their hands blindly in a hole to grab a lobster, accidentally putting their fingers or hand in the moray's mouth.

There is a myth that once a moray bites it will not let go until its head is cut off. Since morays breathe by taking water through their mouth and pumping it out their gills, they would quickly die if they did not let go after biting.

At some dive sites, divers actually hand feed morays. Keep in mind that if you do this, there is always the risk that the moray could accidentally bite you as it attempts to get the food.

Moray eels are found all over the world.

Octopuses are highly intelligent

The octopus is a highly intelligent creature that spends much of its time hiding in holes. It is not aggressive and will usually do its best to avoid contact with people. It can be easily injured by rough handling.

To disguise itself, the octopus is a master of color change and camouflage. Unless you know what you are looking for, or unless the animal moves, you may pass right over an octopus and not even know that it is there.

Most octopuses are rather small, ranging from a few inches in length to several feet. The only exception are the giant octopuses that live in the Pacific northwest, which may grow to lengths in excess of 20 feet.

Every octopus has a beak on its underside which it uses for feeding. This "jaw" can inflict a painful wound if the octopus is large, however, it is rare to hear of a diver being bitten.

In Australia, the small blue ringed octopus delivers a deadly neurotoxin with its bite. Snorkelers should avoid handling these animals.

Most octopuses are rather small, usually not over a foot or two in length.

Sea urchins look like underwater porcupines

Sea urchins probably cause more injuries to divers than any other marine creature. Although they don't swim, and crawl so slowly that you'll barely notice their movement, divers frequently brush against them or step on them, injuring both the sea urchin and themselves.

Sea urchins are "invertebrates", which are animals without backbones. These animals do not have a brain. Urchins are primitive creatures that feed primarily on plants, but can also filter out other matter from the water surrounding them.

The spines of the sea urchin are pointy and hard, but brittle. If you accidentally run into a sea urchin the spines may break off under your skin. This can lead to an infection and with repeated contact, you may develop a sensitivity to them. While in most cases the spines will dissolve on their own, you may want to see a doctor to have them removed, particularly if they are deep under the skin or it appears an infection is developing.

The sea urchins that are found along the west coast and off the northeast coast of the U.S. are considered a delicacy in Japan and are called "uni" in sushi bars. Only the yellow roe is eaten after it has been removed from inside the animal. You can mix the roe with sour cream and make a tasty seafood dip.

Sea urchins move slowly and rely on their spines to defend themselves from predators.

Jellyfish aren't really fish

Jellyfish aren't really fish, but colonies of thousands of tiny animals that live together cooperatively. Although they have the ability to swim, their movements carry them up and down through the water column, rather than from place to place.

Most jellyfish have stinging cells that can cause skin irritation similar to a burn. If you are diving in waters where jellyfish are known to be present, wearing a wetsuit or a dive skin is a good idea.

Jellyfish are not aggressive creatures, they merely drift with the tides. However, you must be alert in the waters where they are present to avoid swimming into them accidentally. The worst thing you could do would be to surface beneath the tentacles of one of the more dangerous species of jellyfish, which is another reason why you need to look up while surfacing.

If you are stung by a jellyfish, the treatment for mild stings is to wash the tentacles off with vinegar. A cortisone based cream may help to relieve the pain.

Some species of jellyfish produce more serious stings that can cause death. These include the Portuguese man-of-war which is found in many tropical seas, and the box jellyfish or "sea wasp" of Australia. Stings from these creatures are extremely dangerous and immediate medical care should be sought. Fortunately, encounters with these creatures are relatively rare and the protection of a dive skin is sufficient to avoid problems in most cases.

Jellyfish drift with the tides. Their pulsing movements are beautiful to watch.
(© Bob Evans/La Mer Bleu Productions. All rights reserved.)

Corals grow slowly

The tiny polyps that build coral reefs are slow workers. It takes them many years to build even a small piece of coral. These creatures are extremely sensitive to silt and other forms of pollution.

In most parts of the world where there are coral reefs, dive boat operators have installed permanent moorings so they do not have to anchor and can avoid damaging the reef. This is essential to the long term health of the reef.

You must be cautious in swimming around coral reefs. Not only can the coral be damaged if you brush against it, but it can also cut you. Coral cuts and scrapes can easily become infected and are frequently slow to heal.

Fire coral, which is easily recognized by its mustard yellow color, is extremely painful to touch and produces serious skin irritation. If you touch fire coral with unprotected skin you will know it instantly.

Fire coral can produce painful skin irritation.

Bristle worms look like large woolly caterpillars

Bristle worms are large marine worms, that have "hairs" or "bristles" sticking out from their bodies. They resemble red and green woolly caterpillars except they grow much larger, in some cases up to a foot in length. Bristle worms are found crawling on corals along the bottom, although occasionally they may be floating in the water.

Bristle worms are not aggressive creatures and all contact between them and snorkelers is always accidental. When bristle worms are touched, the bristles instantly become erect and easily penetrate human skin. The bristles are extremely painful and should be removed, if possible, with either a pair of tweezers or by using adhesive tape. The pain from contact with a bristle worm will usually subside within a few hours, but may last up to two days.

Bristle worms are beautiful, but should not be touched.

There are always new things to see underwater

Keep in mind that this chapter has only provided an introduction to some of the more interesting and common marine creatures. There are thousands of different types of fish and undersea creatures and every area of the world holds new species. Even marine biologists who have been diving all over the world for many years encounter new creatures regularly. You may be the first to discover some new underwater creature that has never been seen before.

CHAPTER 10

SNORKELING ACTIVITIES

While the mere act of swimming on the surface or underwater with mask, fins, and snorkel can be exhilarating, the true adventure of snorkeling is in the many things that your equipment will allow you to do. Whether you choose to watch fish, take photographs, explore shipwrecks, or collect shells, your snorkeling gear will provide the means to do all of these things.

Fish watching is an art

Fish watching is one of the most fascinating aspects of snorkeling! It will be a part of every day you spend in the water, even if you are more interested in other activities like shipwreck exploration. There will almost always be fish around you while you are snorkeling, and in most cases, their antics are just too interesting to ignore.

While certain species of fish will allow you to approach them quite closely, to many fish you will appear as a large, imposing creature that should be avoided. If you want to get close to marine life, you must learn to move as quietly through the water as possible.

Fish exhibit many interesting behaviors and there is endless variety in their shapes and colors.

The more you know about marine creatures and their habits, the easier you will find it to get close to certain species. For example, if you want to see a halibut, a large flatfish that lives on sandy bottoms, you need to know enough not to bother spending too much time looking for them on rocky reefs. If you want to watch a trumpet fish in the Caribbean, you need to look for them hiding in sea whips.

When identifying fish, it's important to look at their shape, size, and colors. There are waterproof fish identification cards that you can take in the water with you that are very helpful for this purpose. To learn about the habits and lives of fish, there are also many excellent field guides you can buy that provide more detailed information on the species you are most likely to see.

Underwater photography lets you share your adventures

Underwater photography is a tremendously rewarding and satisfying way to capture your snorkeling adventures. It's also a great way to share your experiences with friends and family who don't participate in snorkeling.

Underwater cameras vary from extremely simple, to highly sophisticated systems capable of capturing magazine quality images. Yet, under the proper conditions, you can create great underwater photos with basic equipment.

The two main types of underwater camera systems are self-contained cameras and "housings." A self-contained underwater camera is designed to go underwater with no additional exterior protection. The entire camera may be submerged because it is watertight. Cameras like this are sold by companies like Sea & Sea and Nikon.

These self-contained underwater cameras require no external case to go under water. They are lightweight and compact.

The advantages of self-contained underwater cameras are that they are usually quite compact and have special lenses designed specifically for underwater use. The disadvantage of these systems is that they tend to be expensive, especially if you already own a good quality topside camera system. Disposable self-contained underwater cameras are also available, but these tend to be rather limited in regards to how deep you can take them underwater.

Housings include waterproof cases or heavy-duty flexible bags that have special seals to keep water out. There are housings available for many of the more popular models of 35 mm cameras as well as for many models of disposable cameras. If you own a high quality 35mm camera system, you may want to consider a housing if you get serious about underwater photography.

Housings for 35mm cameras are available for the more popular models.

Inexpensive underwater camera options include housings for disposable cameras, waterproof disposable cameras, and flexible bag housing for point-and-shoot cameras.

    The advantage of a housing is that if you own a quality 35mm camera, you can save some money rather than investing in a completely separate underwater system. The disadvantage of a housing is that they tend to be rather large, bulky, and heavy. There are also housings available for certain digital cameras.

    No matter what type of underwater camera system you select, you must take the time to read the owner's manual at least once, and prepare the camera properly prior to each dive. Every underwater camera is dependent on round rubber "o-rings" which are used to seal the water out of these cameras. Your owner's manual will explain where the o-rings need to go and how to maintain them. There are also internal o-rings that you will not be able to access that must be serviced annually by an underwater-camera repairman.

Without properly maintained o-rings in place, the camera will flood, ruining the camera and the film. All underwater cameras have at least one user-serviceable o-ring and some have as many as three or four. The o-rings are normally lubricated with a light coating of special grease prior to each use, and they must be kept free of dirt, sand, hair, or other foreign matter. A single hair trapped below an o-ring can cause an underwater camera to leak.

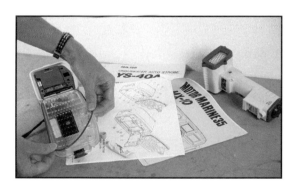

Almost all underwater camera systems use o-rings to seal the case or housing. These must be properly lubricated and installed in the camera prior to every dive.

If your skin diving abilities develop to the point where you can hold your breath and descend to depths greater than twenty feet, and you are serious about underwater photography, eventually you will want an electronic underwater flash. Electronic flash lighting is essential to capture color and detail in underwater photos any time you are shooting more than a few feet below the surface.

One of the keys to successful underwater photography is to get as close to your subject as possible before you trigger the shutter. Ideally, you should never be further than 3-5 feet away from any subject you intend to photograph underwater. At distances further than this, any particles in the water will tend to make your subject look less than sharp and the colors will tend to be dull. Most serious underwater photographers use wide angle lenses, ranging from 13mm to 24mm, to allow them to get close to large subjects underwater.

An electronic underwater flash will help you restore color in your underwater photos.

You must be as motionless as possible when you operate the shutter on your camera. Faster shutter speeds will allow for some movement on your part, but can only be used when there is sufficient light to do so. The minimum shutter speed that should be used in most situations underwater is 1/60 of a second.

Use ISO 400 film for shooting prints underwater. This film is quite forgiving of mistakes in exposure. Use ISO 100 or higher film for shooting transparencies (slides).

Shoot horizontal subjects, such as a dolphin in the horizontal mode. Don't be afraid to turn the camera vertically to capture vertical underwater subjects, such as another snorkeler surfacing from a dive. Fill the frame with your subject whenever possible and don't waste your time or your film shooting photos of subjects that are far away.

In clear water, with lots of sunshine, underwater photography is relatively easy. However, if the water is murky or there is little sun, underwater photography becomes much more difficult. To take top quality underwater photographs takes many years of practice and dedication.

You must be as motionless as possible when you take an underwater photo.

Proper maintenance of your underwater photography equipment is essential. Most dive boats will have a rinse bucket available for rinsing your equipment after you have been in the water. If you have good quality equipment, make sure you only rinse it in a bucket or tub that has been set aside solely for cameras.

If there are multiple camera systems aboard, don't let your camera get placed in the bottom of the bucket with multiple cameras on top of it. This is a sure way for your system to be damaged. You can use almost anything that will hold water, such as a trash can or cooler, as a rinse bucket. If the boat does not have adequate rinsing facilities, take your own container, or keep your camera in a trash can or bucket filled with salt water until you can soak it in fresh water.

Your camera should be rinsed and soaked in fresh water within five minutes of it coming out of salt water. Do not allow your camera to dry with salt water on it as the salts will dry and damage the internal o-rings and camera mechanisms. The camera should be soaked for a minimum of 20-30 minutes or longer if possible.

Underwater cameras and housings should be serviced on an annual basis by an authorized repair technician to avoid potential problems. Without annual service, you risk flooding your camera.

Underwater video is easy

Underwater video is much easier than underwater photography and even a novice underwater videographer can get fantastic results immediately. This is because video actually sees even better than the human eye does underwater!

Video cameras are much more sensitive to light than most film, allowing you to capture scenes under a wide variety of conditions. With underwater video you can capture the movement and behavior of fish in a way that is not possible with still photographs.

There are no self-contained underwater video systems, so any camera you select must be used in a housing. The most compact housings are available for the most compact cameras, such as High-band 8 cameras and digital video cameras.

Like housings for underwater still cameras, video housings are also dependent on o-rings to provide watertight seals underwater. You must be just as careful in preparing a video housing for underwater use as you would be in preparing a still camera.

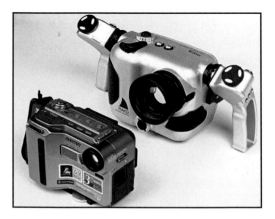

Underwater video housings are extremely compact and easy to use.
(Photo courtesy Light and Motion Industries)

With most video cameras you will be able to see exactly what you are filming as you are recording it. The most important thing for the new video cameraman to remember is to move the camera slowly and smoothly so that the person who watches the finished tape can understand what they are seeing. When you move the camera quickly in jerky movements it is difficult for people to follow the action.

Lights can help brighten video shot at depth, but for shallow water work, in less than 20 feet of water, they are entirely unnecessary. If lights are used, they need to be on adjustable arms that allow you to position them effectively.

Video housings must be maintained like any underwater camera or housing. A good soaking in fresh water is essential after each use.

Spearfishing is challenging

Spearfishing has been a popular sport since the 1940s, and it is an exciting way to capture your own dinner underwater. To dive and land your own fish underwater is both challenging and rewarding. Nothing beats the taste of a freshly speared fish that you have gotten yourself.

Spearfishermen can select from many different types of spearguns and pole spears. The type of gear you use will be determined by where you plan to hunt, what fish you plan to hunt, and how much money you want to spend.

Pole spears are the simplest way to get started in underwater hunting, as well as the least expensive. A pole spear consists of a shaft or "pole", with a ring of rubber surgical tubing at one end and a spear tip at the other. To use a pole spear you simply grasp the surgical tubing in the gap between the thumb and forefinger of your dominant hand, and stretch the tubing by thrusting the shaft behind you using your free hand. Grab the shaft with the same hand that holds the tubing and hold it firmly. Aim the shaft at the fish you intend to spear and when you release the shaft, the pole spear will leap forward, hopefully impaling the fish. Using a pole spear takes skill and practice.

Spearguns use several different types of mechanisms to propel their shafts, but the most common are band-powered guns and pneumatic guns. Both types are quite effective, although band guns are the most common.

The simplest underwater spear is the pole spear.

Band guns use rubber "bands" made from surgical tubing that is stretched from the muzzle at the front of the gun and attach to the shaft near the rear of the gun. A trigger mechanism holds the spear in the gun until the trigger is pulled and the shaft is released. The gun itself may be made of wood or aluminum.

Band guns come in different sizes, and the larger the gun the more difficult it is to load. As you might expect, small guns are usually used to shoot small fish. Larger guns are used for bigger fish or at longer distances for fish that are difficult to approach.

There are many different tricks and techniques that will make you a more effective underwater hunter. For example, knowing which fish respond to an incoming tide or an ebb tide is useful. Understanding where your shot must hit the fish is essential.

Successful underwater hunters learn how to use the terrain and temperature "breaks" in the ocean to their advantage. They learn to take advantage of the feeding and breeding behaviors of different species of fish.

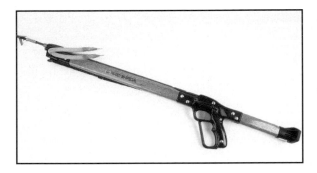

Band guns are the most commonly used type of speargun.

Most tropical diving resorts do not allow spearfishing and some islands, such as Grand Cayman, completely prohibit the importation of spearguns. In California, there are laws which govern all forms of fishing, including spearfishing. Most inland states do not allow spearfishing for anything but "rough" fish like carp or catfish. Be sure to check local regulations before you go spearfishing. Buy a license and observe all applicable laws. Most dive stores will be able to fill you in on the local requirements, protected species, and good places to hunt.

Spearfishing is very popular in California.

To become a good spearfisherman takes many years of practice and dedication. You must learn the habits of the fish that you hunt, and you must develop your breath-hold capabilities to a high degree. The most productive spearfishermen have learned to think like a fish!

All good spearfishermen practice conservation and only take enough fish to feed their immediate family. Underwater hunters who are greedy, waste fish, or take game that is small, undersized, or out of season are looked upon poorly by other sportsmen.

Catching lobsters

Snorkeling and catching lobsters is great fun and provides a delicious dinner, if you are successful. Lobster is always a special treat, whether cooked on the barbecue, in the broiler, boiled, or steamed in a clam bake.

There are different species of lobsters in almost every part of the world, but the basic habits of these animals are the same. They tend to live in holes or crevices in the reef, inside shipwrecks, inside broken pipes, or any secluded location they can find. They tend to stay inside their homes during the daylight hours, but venture out onto the reef to feed at night.

During the fall months, in California, lobsters can be found in extremely shallow water, hiding in the eel grass, where they mate. When the water is clear off the beach, lobster diving in California can be excellent in water as shallow as six feet or less.

Lobster diving regulations vary from region to region. In California, for example, lobsters may only be caught by hand and the season normally runs from early October to mid-March. In Florida, divers may use a "tickle" stick to coax the lobster into a net, or they may use a snare, but these items are strictly forbidden in California. On most islands in the Caribbean, it is illegal for tourists to hunt for lobsters.

A flashlight is a handy accessory for hunting for lobsters, even during daylight hours, since the lobsters hide in holes. Many snorkelers prefer to look for lobsters at night when the lobsters are out in the open and much easier to catch.

Most lobsters you will approach underwater during the daytime will be sitting at the opening to a hole with their antennae pointed outward. They are extremely wary creatures and will bolt the moment they think you are behaving aggressively.

To catch a California lobster by hand, one technique is to use one hand to distract the lobster by slowly wiggling your fingers at a short distance in front of it. With your free hand, make a fast grab for the main body or "carapace" of the lobster. Pin the lobster to the floor of its hole and use your free hand to gain a second, firmer grip. Swim the lobster to the surface where you can take your time getting the lobster into your bag.

Lobsters are found in almost all parts of the world. This diver is holding a California spiny lobster.

Lobsters are easy to clean once they have been cooked. Simply split them down the middle, lengthwise, remove the intestinal tract, rinse, and enjoy!

Hunting for abalone

One of the great delicacies of the world is the abalone, a large, flattened marine snail that lives in California, Canada, Australia, South Africa, and other parts of the world. When properly prepared, abalone is one of the tastiest creatures in the sea.

Skin diving for abalone in northern California is an extremely popular activity for divers from all over the state. The red abalone which grows there reaches lengths of over 10 inches. These creatures are found on rocky ledges where they feed on kelp and other algae.

Abalone have no protection other than their thick shell and the tremendous suction they can generate by clamping down with their muscular foot. They have no coagulant in their blood, so if they are accidentally cut they will bleed to death.

To take an abalone you must have an approved abalone "iron" or "bar," a measuring device, and a fishing license with the proper stamp. The iron is a large, curved pry bar with rounded edges that will not cut or injure the abalone in any way. You will also need a catch bag and a surface float of some type to hold your abalone while you continue to skin dive.

Look at your measuring device carefully before you dive and learn to estimate the size of an abalone shell so that you don't waste time and energy popping undersize animals. Every time you take an undersize abalone you risk injuring the animal, causing it to die.

When an abalone is relaxed its shell is raised up off the rock and you can see the "mantle" or frilly tentacles sticking out from the sides of the shell. This is the time to slide your

Abalone may only be taken by skin divers in Northern California.

abalone iron under the foot of the abalone, with the tip of the iron against the rock. Once the iron is under the shell, lift the handle of the iron and pry the abalone off the rock.

Measure the abalone immediately, and if it is under-sized, put it back in the same spot you found it, with its foot against the rock, until it holds on by itself. Never drop an abalone from the surface to the bottom, because every fish in the area will immediately attack and devour it.

To clean an abalone it must be shucked from its shell using a flat, wooden, shucking tool, which is sold at most dive stores. Trim the dark meat and intestines carefully away from the foot and slice the abalone into thin steaks, preferably no more than 1/8 inch thick. Be sure to carefully feel the stomach of the abalone for any hard spots which might indicate the presence of an abalone pearl. These can be beautiful!

Tenderize the meat with a mallet and you're ready to cook your catch. Abalone can be sautéed, deep fried, or pre-pared in many other ways. One personal favorite is Abalone Relleño. To make this treat, wrap an abalone steak around a mild green chili pepper and some cheese, skewer it with a wooden toothpick, batter it, and deep fry. Enjoy!

Save the shell of the abalone and clean the marine growth off the back with a stiff wire brush. The interior of the abalone shell is an iridescent mother of pearl and is especially beautiful. Store the shell outside until the smell goes away. Abalone shells make wonderful gifts and people are delighted to have them.

Shell collecting is another way to bring home a memory of every trip

Shells are found in both fresh and salt water, although the widest variety and most colorful shells are found in the sea. Shells vary in size from the giant tridacna clam found in the Indo-Pacific region to extremely tiny shells like the miniature horn shell found in the Caribbean.

Shells are formed by marine creatures who use them as their homes and for protection from predators. Although some shells will vary in color depending upon what the animal has eaten, most shells have specific color schemes.

Look for shells anywhere you dive, but especially in the sandy area at the edge of a reef, in pockets of sand or cuts between reefs, and on the reef itself. Conservation minded shell collectors only take dead shells, not living shells with animals inside them. Most live shells will be recognized by either the animal that lives in the shell itself or by the presence of the "trap door" or "operculum," a separate oval piece of shell attached to the animal's body, which the animal uses to help defend itself from attack.

Dead shells will frequently provide a home for hermit crabs that take over a shell when the animal that formed the shell dies. Hermit crabs are easily recognized by their claws, their hairy appearance, and their rapid movements, which are not characteristic of the animals that normally inhabit shells.

You can learn more about shell collecting from the many guide books that are available on the subject. There are also "malacological" societies of shell collectors in most large coastal cities, who meet to discuss shell collecting and rare finds.

There are beautiful shells underwater in almost every part of the world. This is a conch shell from the Caribbean.

SNORKELING FUN

Wreck diving offers history and adventure

For many snorkelers, swimming over a sunken wreck is one of the most exciting underwater activities imaginable. Wrecks offer a glimpse into the past, as well as mystery and adventure.

While it's every diver's dream to find an untouched wreck, loaded with gold doubloons, this is rarely the case. Most wrecks in shallow water have been discovered, although as storms churn the sands of the beach, previously undiscovered wrecks are occasionally exposed.

Most wrecks in U.S. waters are protected by the Abandoned Shipwreck Act of 1988 which prohibits the removal of artifacts from any wreck fifty years old or older. The penalties for violating this law are stiff. If you're in doubt as to the legality of removing an item from a shipwreck, don't take a chance, leave the item where it lies. This will also give other snorkelers a chance to see and enjoy these artifacts. Shipwrecks in foreign countries are also usually protected, particularly if they have any historical value.

Exploring a shipwreck becomes most interesting when you know something about the history of the wreck, how it got there, and the lives of the passengers and crew. There are numerous books on shipwrecks written from the diver's perspective, explaining where to go snorkeling and what you will see.

Wrecks are home to many different animals, including encrusting creatures like corals, lobsters, and numerous types of fish. In the Caribbean and other tropical locations it's not uncommon for wrecks to be filled with thousands of tiny brightly colored fish known as "silversides."

As a snorkeler, you must never enter a wreck, due to the risk of becoming lost or trapped inside the wreck. Most wrecks are filled with fine silt that can be stirred up instantly by a careless fin kick. This can reduce underwater visibility to zero inside the wreck. Even scuba divers must be specially trained for wreck "penetration", and many divers have died

Shipwrecks are fascinating to explore.

when they became lost inside a wreck or the wreck collapsed on top of them.

Always wear gloves and some type of protective suit when diving around shipwrecks. The jagged edges of metal found on most wrecks are razor sharp and can cause serious cuts.

Watch out for fishing lines and nets whenever you explore a shipwreck. Wrecks are popular with fishermen and it is not uncommon for them to lose nets or break their lines on a wreck. These can cause entanglement if you are careless and could lead to drowning. For this reason, you should always carry a sharp knife whenever you explore a shipwreck.

One of the best places to snorkel and see lots of shipwrecks is the island of Bermuda off the east coast of the U.S. Excellent wrecks in shallow water are scattered throughout the Caribbean, the Florida Keys, the coast of California, Truk Lagoon, and numerous other sites.

Bottle collecting

Bottle collecting provides another window to the past, in the days when bottles were often made by hand or using primitive molds. Almost any pier can be a likely place to find old bottles, which were often discarded over the side, during the early days of sailing.

Piers are good places to search for bottles because the water around them is frequently shallow and piers in old port towns are where ships offloaded their cargo. In the early days of shipping, some British ships used beer bottles as part of their ballast. These distinctive bottles have been found at many ports.

Ship's decanters can be recognized by their enlarged bottoms and narrow tops, which helped to stabilize them aboard a rocking ship. Some old bottles can be quite valuable.

There are several dangers to diving near piers and wharves that must be considered before you go searching for bottles. Snorkeling in enclosed harbors where there is poor water circulation, is not recommended, due to the strong possibility of dangerous pollutants being present in the water and mud found on the bottom. High levels of bacteria, as well as toxic chemicals from boat bottom paints, are found in most harbors.

Snorkeling near piers where there is any boat traffic is dangerous and in most cases, prohibited by the pier operator. In locations where boats must use the pier for launching or recovering this is especially hazardous.

Since most piers are used for fishing, you can expect to find large amounts of fishing line, hooks, and lures underwater. In many cases, this line is designed to be invisible underwater and can present a serious hazard to snorkelers. Be sure to carry a sharp knife with you and avoid snorkeling around piers where the underwater visibility is poor.

Most bottles found underwater will have some encrusting marine life on the outside of the bottle, as well as the possibility of marine life inside the bottle, too. Living creatures that may be found inside bottles include octopus, clams, fish, and crabs. Be sure to give any creature the chance to exit the bottle before permanently removing the bottle from the water.

All of these bottles were collected underwater off San Diego, California. *(From the bottle collection of Lance Milbrand.)*

CHAPTER 11

WHAT ABOUT SCUBA DIVING?

Scuba diving offers greater opportunities to explore underwater, but also involves a bigger commitment to diving in terms of time, money, and effort. The decision to participate in scuba diving is a personal one that each person must make for himself.

If you are really interested in the diving activities described in the previous chapter, you may decide you want to try scuba diving. Most dive stores and resorts have short, introductory courses to give you a taste of what scuba diving is all about.

It is not difficult to learn to scuba dive or participate in scuba activities. The boats that take scuba divers out to dive typically go to sites that are more remote and deeper than those boats that are oriented towards snorkeling trips. There are live-aboard dive boats that offer week-long trips to deeper dive sites especially for scuba divers. Scuba diving opens up more of the underwater world to your exploration.

Is scuba diving "better" than snorkeling? No, it's just a different type of diving. If you are happy snorkeling in six feet of water, and see all that you want to see there, then you don't need to make the investment in learning to use scuba and buying the equipment to participate. However, if you want to explore shipwrecks in deep water, or you become serious about underwater photography, then you should consider taking the time to learn to use scuba.

If you want to explore deeper waters, you may want to consider scuba diving.

Scuba appeals primarily to people who seek the more adventurous side of underwater exploration. It requires a bit of technical understanding, and you must be responsible for selecting, using, transporting, and maintaining your gear. To many people, this is part of what makes scuba diving interesting. Some divers go beyond ordinary scuba diving into deeper, more advanced diving known as "technical diving". This type of diving involves a very high level of risk.

Professional deep sea diving is the ultimate form of diving, which takes divers to depths as deep as 1600 feet in the open sea. This type of diving requires extensive training, apprenticeship, and a commitment of many years of involvement.

Snorkeling is enough for many

Snorkeling can provide you with many days of adventure and excitement. It's an activity that you can enjoy throughout your life, long after the time you might not feel like lugging heavy scuba tanks around any more.

Snorkeling is a personal activity that is best shared with another partner. It's exploration, nature, tropical islands, sunshine, and clear water all wrapped up into one irresistible package. Enjoy snorkeling!

ABOUT THE AUTHOR

Steve Barsky has been snorkeling and scuba diving for many years. He is experienced in sport, scientific, and commercial diving, and is an avid underwater hunter and photographer.

Steve started diving in 1965 in Los Angeles and became a diving instructor in 1970. His first employment in the industry was with a dive store in Los Angeles, and he went on to work for almost 10 years in the retail dive store environment.

Steve Barsky is a professional underwater photographer and author. (Photo © Kristine Barsky)

He attended the University of California at Santa Barbara, where he earned a Masters Degree in 1976 in Human Factors Engineering. His master's thesis was one of the first to deal with the use of underwater video systems in commercial diving. Steve's work was a pioneering effort at the time and was used by the Navy in developing applications for underwater video systems.

Steve traveled to the North Sea in 1976 and worked as a commercial diver through 1983. He made dives from drill rigs, supply ships, and barges throughout the North Sea, Gulf of Mexico, and along the east coast of the U.S. His deepest working dive was to 580 feet.

In 1983, Steve returned to Santa Barbara to work for Diving Systems International, a manufacturer of commercial diving masks and helmets. He worked in marketing for Diving Systems, producing all of the company's manuals, catalogs, and advertisements. Barsky was marketing manager for Viking America, Inc., an international manufacturer of dry suits.

In 1989, Steve formed Marine Marketing and Consulting, based in Santa Barbara, California. The company provides market research, marketing plans, consulting, newsletters, promotional articles, technical manuals, and other services for the diving and ocean industry. Steve also does diving accident investigation and serves as an expert witness in diving accident litigation.

Steve is an accomplished underwater photographer and author. His photos and articles have been used in numerous magazines. He has also produced equipment catalogs, advertisements, training programs, and textbooks. As a writer and photographer, Barsky's work has been published in *Asian Diver, Sea Technology, Skin Diver, Offshore Magazine, Emergency, Fire Engineering, Dive Training Magazine, Searchlines, Sources, Undersea Biomedical Reports, Santa Barbara Magazine, Scuba Times, Sport Diver, Underwater Magazine, Scuba Diver,* and many other publications.

Steve lives in Santa Barbara, California where he regularly dives the Channel Islands with his wife Kristine, a marine biologist.

INDEX

A

abalone: 143-145;
abalone iron: 144;
abalone pearl: 145;
Abandoned Shipwreck Act of 1988: 147;
accessories: 6, 9, 63;
accidents: 5, 83;
adjustable heel strap: 16, 45;
adventure: 75, 152;
air: 72;
airway: 49;
alcohol: 86;
allergies: 66;
anemones: 96;
angel shark: 118;
apprenticeship: 152;
aquatic plants: 52, 86;
aquatic weeds: 33;
arms: 51;
artifacts: 147;
assistance: 21, 56;
asthma: 6;
attached hood: 44, 58;
Australia: 126, 143;

B

backwards roll: 108;
barracuda: 112;
bathing suit: 3;
beach: 45, 97, 100-102;
beach diving: 97, 103;
beak: 126;
beaver tail: 43, 58;
Bermuda: 148;
blast method of snorkel clearing: 50;
bleeding fish: 120;
blisters: 17;
blood vessels: 66;
blue ringed octopus: 126;
boat: 108;
boaters: 90;
boat diving: 103;
boat operators: 27;
boat traffic: 28, 90, 149;
boogie board: 18, 49, 85;
booties: 16, 42;
bottle: 149;

bottle collecting: 149;
bottom time: 73;
box jellyfish: 128;
breath: 6, 11, 59, 73;
breath-hold dive: 64;
breath-hold diving: 3, 59;
breath-hold time: 73;
briefing: 105;
bubbles: 1;
buckle: 58, 61, 70, 106;
buddy: 9, 20, 43;
buddy system: 21;
buddy team: 70;
buoyancy: 20-23, 25, 62-64;
buoyancy compensator: 7, 19, 29;
buoyancy test: 63;
burn: 27;
bus: 103;
butterfly fish: 93;

C

calf: 61;
calico bass: 94;
California: 89, 101, 141-143, 149;
camera: 52;
Canada: 143;
Caribbean: 92, 112, 117, 142, 146-147, 149;
carp: 141;
cartilaginous fish: 114;
catfish: 141;
chafing: 17;
channel in the sand: 101;
charter boat: 103;
children: 7, 75, 77-78;
clams: 150;
cleaner fish: 93;
clearing your ears: 65;
CO_2 mechanisms: 19;
coagulant: 144;
colors: 35;
commitment: 152;
compressed air: 6;
compressed air tanks: 6;
contact: 78;
contact lenses: 12;
coral: 87, 92, 147;
coral cuts: 129;
coral reef: 92, 128;

corrosion inhibitor: 34;
cortisone based cream: 128;
CPR: 21, 88;
crabs: 96, 150;
cramp: 20, 85-86;
crayfish: 91;
crotch strap: 44, 60;
cuff: 43;
curiosity: 79;
current: 79, 96, 101, 109;
current line: 107;

D

death: 59;
deep water: 151;
defog solutions: 47;
dehydration: 86;
diabetes: 6;
digital video cameras: 138;
dish soap: 12;
displacement method
  of snorkel clearing: 72;
distress: 54;
dive skin: 3, 22;
dive boats: 137;
dive computer: 7;
dive door: 105;
dive flag: 27, 49;
dive knife: 33-34, 61;
dive ladder: 57;
dive light: 33-34, 63;
dive operation: 103;
dive partner: 86;
dive site: 36;
dive skin: 22, 40-41, 58, 83;
dive store: 13, 91, 142, 151;
dive suit: 22;
divemaster: 54, 105;
diving partner: 87;
dizziness (vertigo): 59;
dock: 90;
doctor: 12;
dolphin: 111-113;
drag: 6, 74;
drop path: 60;
drowning: 59, 65, 87, 148;
dry compartments: 36;

E

eardrum: 65-66;
earplugs: 28, 59;
ears: 3, 65, 122;
education: 81;
eel grass: 142;

electronic underwater flash: 135;
emergency: 20;
energy: 6, 84;
entanglement: 86, 148;
equalize: 3, 13;
equipment: 2, 9, 75, 99, 101, 151;
exhaustion: 20, 84, 96;
exit: 100;
experience: 6;
eyes: 13, 66;

F

face: 10, 66;
fairy basslets: 93;
family activity: 75;
Farallon Islands: 119;
farmer-john: 42;
feet first dive: 69;
field guides: 132;
filter feeders: 115, 120;
fins: 1, 2, 9, 15, 39, 52-53, 57, 78, 85,
  87, 97-100, 109;
first aid: 21;
fish: 35, 112, 131, 139-140, 147, 150;
fish watching: 131;
fishing lines: 33, 148-149;
fit: 11;
fitness: 3;
flashlight: 143;
flippers: 15;
flood: 135;
Florida: 112-114, 121;
Florida Keys: 149;
fluids: 80, 86, 105;
Force Fin: 51;
forehead: 54;
forward momentum dive: 69;
free diving: 3;
fresh water: 29, 137;
fresh water springs: 113;
fruit juices: 86;
full foot fin: 15-16, 45, 77;

G

garibaldi: 94;
gate: 105;
gear bag: 36;
giant stride entry: 105;
glare: 78;
glasses: 12;
gloves: 17, 49, 148;
goggles: 13;
goody bag: 37;
Grand Cayman Island: 117, 141;

great barracuda: 121;
Great Lakes: 91;
Great White Shark: 119;
groupers: 93;

H

hair: 11, 48, 78;
halibut: 96;
harbor seals: 119, 122;
Hawaii: 92;
hazard: 97, 149;
head: 63, 71;
hearing loss: 59, 66;
hermit crabs: 146;
High-band 8 cameras: 138;
hip weights: 25;
hood: 23, 25, 44, 49;
hooks: 149;
horn shark: 118;
housing: 133-134, 138;
hyperventilation: 73;

I

infection: 59, 65;
inflatable vest: 18;
inflatables: 103;
injury: 5, 13, 29;
instruction: 3, 6;
instructor: 3;
insulation: 18, 22, 24;
internal diameter: 14;
invertebrates: 126;
Isle Royale National Park: 91;

J

jacket: 41-42, 58;
jellyfish: 127-128;
jet skis: 90;
judgment: 83;

K

kelp: 47, 52-53, 69, 71, 87, 96;
kelp crawling: 53;
kelp dive: 66, 69;
kick: 51;
knee pads: 24;
knife: 62, 87, 148-149;
knife sheaths: 24;
knowledge: 5;

L

lack of oxygen: 76;
ladder: 106, 109;
lake: 91;
lanyard: 36;
lead shot: 26;
lead weight: 25;
legs: 51, 67;
lens: 11, 47;
leopard shark: 118;
license: 141;
lifeguard: 54;
lights: 139;
lines: 86;
lionfish: 124;
live-aboard dive boats: 151;
lobsters: 35, 96, 125, 142-143, 147;
loss of hearing: 65;
lures: 149;
Lycra®: 40;

M

maintenance: 137;
malacological societies: 146;
manatees: 113;
manta rays: 94, 114-115;
marine aquarium: 113;
marine creature: 75, 131;
marine growth: 145;
marine life: 1, 5, 33, 67, 87, 90, 111, 150;
marine life i.d.: 92;
marine life identification books: 92;
Marine Mammal Protection Act: 112;
marine mammals: 112, 119, 122;
mask: 1, 2, 9, 12, 34, 39, 40, 47, 49, 52, 54, 58, 66, 77-78, 84, 87, 98, 106, 108;
mask strap: 108;
measuring device: 144;
mesh gear bag: 36;
middle ear: 59;
miniature horn shell: 145;
model: 20;
molded weights: 26;
money: 151;
moray eels: 124-125;
mother of pearl: 145;
mouthpiece: 49, 74;
mucous: 66;

N

negative buoyancy: 64;
neoprene: 18, 22;

neoprene booties: 16;
neoprene socks: 16;
nets: 33, 86, 148;
neurotoxin: 126;
Nikon: 133;
nose: 13;
nostrils: 65;
nurse shark: 118;
nylon: 24, 27;
nylon webbing: 25;

O

o-ring grease: 35;
o-rings: 35, 135, 137-138;
ocean: 92, 97-98;
octopus: 125-126, 150;
open heel adjustable fins: 17, 77;
open water: 77-78;
operculum: 146;
optical quality: 12;
overheating: 44;
owner's manual: 134;
oxygen: 73;

P

pain: 66;
panic: 87;
pants: 42, 58;
parrotfish: 94;
pelagics: 94;
personal flotation device: 18;
personal needs: 24;
personal watercraft: 90;
physical ailments: 6;
physical condition: 3, 6;
physical effort: 84;
physical fitness: 2;
piers: 149;
pike dive: 66, 69;
ping pong ball: 15;
plan: 96;
plankton: 115, 120;
plastic lens: 12;
pneumatic guns: 140;
pockets: 36;
pole spears: 139;
pollutants: 149;
polyps: 92, 94, 128;
pool: 78;
Portuguese Man-of-War: 128;
positive buoyancy: 64, 84, 88;
potato: 47;
practice: 73;
precautions: 75;

prescription lenses: 13;
pressure: 5, 59, 65-66;
pressure gauge: 7;
professional deep sea diving: 152;
propulsion: 17, 67;
protected species: 113;
pups: 122;

Q

quick release buckle: 26;

R

razor edge: 34;
reef: 34;
regulations: 141;
regulator: 7, 39;
rental costs: 7;
repair technician: 138;
resorts: 151;
right hand release: 60;
rip currents: 101;
risks: 5, 152;
river: 91;
rocks: 97, 103;
roe: 127;
rookeries: 119;
rubber seal: 10;

S

safe boat operation: 90;
safe diving practices: 83;
safety: 84;
safety rules: 87;
Safety Sausage: 56;
saliva: 47;
salt water: 18;
San Miguel Island: 119;
sand: 97, 103;
sand dollars: 96;
sandy bottoms: 115;
scuba: 1, 6, 17, 151;
scuba divers: 105, 148;
scuba diving: 3, 6-7, 151;
scuba tanks: 152;
Scuba Tuba: 56;
Sea & Sea: 133;
sea conditions: 96;
sea lions: 96, 111-112, 119, 122;
sea otters: 111;
sea urchin: 126;
sea wasp: 128;
sea whips: 93;
seals: 96, 122;

seasickness: 103;
self-contained underwater breathing apparatus: 6;
self-contained underwater camera: 133;
self-draining valves: 50;
serrated edge: 34;
shade: 31;
shallow water blackout: 74;
shark: 115, 117, 119;
sheephead: 94;
shell: 131, 145-146;
shell collectors: 146-147;
ship channel: 90;
ship's decanters: 149;
shipwrecks: 2, 33-34, 81, 87, 91, 131, 142, 147, 151;
shucking tool: 145;
shutter speed: 136;
signal: 55;
silt: 147;
silversides: 93, 147;
skill level: 6;
skills: 21, 35;
skin: 3;
skin diver: 1, 62, 67;
skin diving: 3, 7, 75, 83, 87;
snorkel: 1, 2, 9, 13, 15, 39-40, 49-50, 53, 63, 72, 77, 86-87, 98;
snorkel keeper: 15, 39;
snorkel tension: 49;
snorkeler: 1;
snorkeling: 7, 17, 75, 83, 106;
snorkeling gear: 131;
snorkeling partner: 106;
snorkeling site: 92, 101, 104;
snorkeling vest: 19, 29, 44, 60, 74, 84, 88;
soft drinks: 86;
South Africa: 143;
spearfisherman: 33;
spearfishing: 120, 139;
spearguns: 63, 139, 141;
spine pads: 24;
spines: 124;
spit: 47;
sponges: 93;
spotted drums: 94;
state laws: 113;
stinging cells: 127;
Stingray City: 117, 121;
stingrays: 96, 114-115, 117;
strap: 11, 48, 58;
stream: 91;
streamlining: 87;
suction: 66;
sun: 6, 18, 31, 83, 90;

sunburn: 83;
surf: 90, 97-101, 103;
surf entry: 97;
surf exits: 100;
surf line: 100;
surf zone: 97, 99;
surface: 13, 19, 21, 49, 51, 59, 71-73;
surface dives: 66-67;
surface diving: 64;
surface flotation: 9, 18;
surfboard: 97;
surfers: 97;
surgical tubing: 139;
sweat: 86;
swell shark: 118;
swim step: 105;
swimmers: 90, 97;
swimming ability: 87;

T

T-shirt: 83;
technical diving: 152;
techniques: 3;
teeth: 112, 122;
tempered glass: 10, 12;
tempered lens: 77;
tentacles: 128;
throat: 65;
tickle stick: 142;
tiger sharks: 119;
tobacco: 47;
Tomales Bay: 119;
torpedo ray: 121;
toxic chemicals: 149;
training: 5, 6, 152;
treasures: 37;
tridacna clam: 145;
trigger mechanism: 140;
triggerfish: 94;
tropical diving: 22;
tropical diving resorts: 141;
tropical seas: 121;
tropical waters: 84;
Truk Lagoon: 149;
trumpet fish: 132;
tuck dive: 66-67;
tunas: 94;

U

undertow: 102;
underwater: 59;
underwater blackout: 5;
underwater cameras: 63, 81, 133, 135;
underwater exploration: 152;

underwater photograph: 136-137;
underwater photography: 5, 117, 132, 135-137, 151;
underwater video: 138;
underwater-camera repairman: 135;
urine: 86;

V

valve: 14, 19, 30, 49;
Velcro®: 42;
video housings: 139;
vinegar: 128;
visibility: 71, 87, 89, 91, 148-149;
viz: 90;

W

waist: 60;
waist strap: 44;
waterproof cases: 133;
waterproof marking pen: 28;
waterproof sunblock: 83;
waves: 79, 90, 98, 100;
WD40®: 34;
weather: 44, 90, 105;
weight: 62-64, 74, 88;
weight belt: 6-7, 25-26, 36, 60, 64, 70-71, 80, 84, 87-88;
weight belt buckles: 26;
weight keepers: 26;
wetsuit: 6, 7, 22, 24-25, 41, 58, 60, 63-64, 80, 83, 114;
wetsuit hanger: 31;
wetsuit jackets: 43;
wetsuits: 80;
whale: 3, 96, 111-112;
whale shark: 94, 120;
wharves: 149;
whistle: 34, 56;
white sharks: 119;
wide angle lenses: 136;
wire brush: 145;
wounds: 111;

Y

Yucatan Peninsula: 121;

Z

zipper: 40.